D0072473

STRATEGIES IN

SOCIAL WORK CONSULTATION

From Theory to Practice
in the Mental Health Field

BOWLING GREEN STATE UNIVERSITY DISCARDED LIBRARY

BOWLING GREEN STATE
UNIVERSITY LIBRARIES

DWIGHT W. RIEMAN

University of Missouri–Columbia

Longman
New York & London

Strategies in Social Work Consultation: From Theory to Practice in the Mental Health Field

Copyright © 1992 by Longman Publishing Group.
All rights reserved.
No part of this publication may be reproduced,
stored in a retrieval system, or transmitted
in any form or by any means, electronic, mechanical,
photocopying, recording, or otherwise,
without the prior permission of the publisher.

Longman, 95 Church Street, White Plains, N.Y. 10601

Associated companies:
Longman Group Ltd., London
Longman Cheshire Pty., Melbourne
Longman Paul Pty., Auckland
Copp Clark Pitman, Toronto

Senior editor: David J. Estrin
Development editor: Elsa Van Bergen
Production editor: Marie-Josée A. Schorp
Cover design: Thomas Phon, Thomas Phon Graphics
Text art: Fine Line, Inc.
Production supervisor: Richard C. Bretan

Library of Congress Cataloging-in-Publication Data

Rieman, Dwight W.
    Strategies in social work consultation: from theory to practice in
the mental health field/Dwight Walker Rieman.
        p.   cm.
    Includes index.
    ISBN 0-8013-0394-X: $31.95
    1. Social service. 2. Social service—United States. 3. Mental health
consultation—United States. I. Title.
HV40.R525   1991
362.2'0425—dc20   90-24752
                                                                        CIP

1 2 3 4 5 6 7 8 9 10-MA-9594939291

Contents

Foreword

I have known the author of this book for a very long time—since his days as a consultant and chief psychiatric social worker in the Texas Department of Mental Health and Mental Retardation. I have known him as a highly skilled practitioner with vast knowledge of national mental health trends and needs and an empathetic understanding of how mental health crises have impacted the lives of people in our varied communities. I have known him as a doer and a motivator who engenders support for mental health initiatives and for a recognition of the many complexities associated with such interventions at multiple levels. I have not, up to now, known him as a writer. What a treat to discover that he has accomplished a work of supreme craftsmanship, reflecting his vast knowledge and experience. This book is especially valuable because it provides a broad as well as in-depth analysis of the consultant's role and the contributions and limits of that role in the mental health arena. Dwight Rieman has provided a valuable document to present and future scholars and practitioners.

This book represents the accomplishment of a most difficult task: to compile an overview of the conceptual underpinnings, the specific techniques, and the emotional qualities necessary for excellence in mental health consultation, both art and science, and to present it in a highly readable and clear form. The book is useful to this and the next generation of social workers, nurses, psychologists, educators, physicians and other professionals and paraprofessionals, as well as clients, their families, and their supporters, who must continue to struggle with one of the most pressing problems of our existence as human beings—the mental dysfunctioning of large numbers of our friends, family members, associates, neighbors, and acquaintances who share existence with us in our journey through life. The book can certainly be used by scholars and teachers in all of the mental health disciplines as a valuable source of information, research, and practice wisdom for the training of students who will soon not only be utilizing the skills of consultants, but also be consultants themselves. At present more good texts on consultation are sorely needed and this book provides a rich treasure for us. Case materials illustrating consultation dilemmas and strategies of resolution are especially helpful as educational aides. The book can also be of value to those who wish to utilize consultation services properly.

Sections of this work are especially helpful because so little information is available to guide the educator and practitioner on these subjects. Recommended sections include those on "The Contract," "Ethics in Consultation" and "Education for Consultation." The "Contract" section is most useful in providing an outline of what should be included in a typical contract between consultant and client. The chapter on "Ethics" discusses the ethical considerations involved in contracting and provides clear examples of ethical decisions, illustrated in the case materials found in other sections of the book. These capture "operational ethical principles" and convey the nuances and sometimes overlooked aspects of ethical concerns in consultation. Especially helpful are descriptions and resolutions of the "in-process" ethical dilemmas that the author himself confronted in managing his own consultation services to client organizations. The Chapter on "Education for Consultation—Refining and Enlarging the Effort" is especially interesting to the academician because it provides a clear picture of the contributions and the lack thereof of the educational establishment. The chapter not only documents the lack of relevant courses and course content on consultation in social work but also provides a wealth of sources for defining and guiding such course construction for those who wish to make such courses available on their campuses. The author himself has certainly made his own contributions in this area at the University of Missouri, but he has greatly added to the source material through this book—a much needed and competently written treatise that will, I am certain, be used for many years as a valuable source of information and case material.

In summary, I am most impressed with Dwight Rieman's contribution to the literature. This book can be used, in whole or in part, for many purposes: education, continuing education, staff training, organizational improvement, and research. The book provides a wealth of insights and realistically documents consultation efforts that can guide others who wish to embark on similar professional endeavors. I congratulate the author for devoting so many of his years to the field of mental health; without those years of service, this book would not have been possible. The book stands as a testament to those many years of dedication and commitment.

Martha S. Williams
Dean
School of Social Work
The University of Texas at Austin

Preface

Consultation is an invaluable method for improving design, delivery, and extension of diagnostic, remedial, and educational efforts for at-risk and other populations in need of mental health and other services. Yet, in spite of its importance, many social workers and other professionals are ill equipped to teach or utilize consultation. A significant contribution to this problem is that the practice is undertaught in most academic programs and continuing education on the job is unavailable or inadequate.

The deficit in preparation is largely due to lack of commitment on the part of educators and agency executives to this relatively new specialty, and to limited references on the subject. In particular, literature and case recordings on method, execution, evaluation, and ethical aspects of the practice are quite sparse.

A major objective of this book is to offer a hands-on guide for consultation through a sample of the experiences of a social worker/mental health consultant, along with varied practical applications from the literature on purposes, principles, and problems of consultation practice. While understanding, provision, and use of consultation have been related primarily to mental health work, many of those skills and experiences are directly applicable to other human service organizations.

A second objective is to encourage stronger teaching, provision, and use of consultation as a means of improving mental health and related efforts in meeting needs for enlarged preventive, remedial, and educational services.

Professional experiences from which this text are drawn began in the Federal Employee Mental Health Clinic, U.S. Public Health Service, Washington, D.C., where I had the good fortune to work for four years as a clinician and consultant. This was a facility ahead of its time in operational philosophy and practice, offering a well-balanced ratio of approximately 50 percent clinical assistance and 50 percent consultation and educational services for government agencies. Both activities, but especially the latter, were concerned with mental health in the industry of government and were directed toward improving the emotional climate in the work place to strengthen employee efficiency, morale, and retention.

This period of rewarding professional growth was followed by an extended one in Texas, first in the State Department of Health, Division of Mental Health, and later in the State Department of Mental Health as consultant and chief psychiatric social worker. Primary responsibilities in both cases were in community development of mental health services and design and staffing of a wide range of in-service training activities for care-giving personnel, including public health nurses, physicians, welfare staff, teachers, corrections employees, and the clergy on the mental health components of their work.

Both of these assignments plus earlier ones in a family agency, state mental hospital, and army neuropsychiatric unit, provided preparation for an appointment in extension and continuing education at the School of Social Work, University of Missouri–Columbia. Consultation and direction there of two major in-service training projects for the Missouri Department of Mental Health offered rich opportunities to extend and consolidate learnings about consultation practice and teaching of the subject.

Fortunately, too, my work as clinician, community organizer, consultant, and educator occurred during periods of significant national mental health history, capsulated in the following developments:

- The visionary but limited national mental health act which provided modest priming of states and territories for prevention, research, and education in the late 1940s and 1950s.
- The exciting and long overdue community mental health services movement of the 1960s and 1970s with its impressive organization of over 700 mental health centers (only half of the national goal).
- The dramatic and distressing retrenchment of federal leadership and funding from mental health and other human services in the 1980s, while emotional, health, and economic problems continued to mount, approaching epidemic proportions of substance abuse, AIDS, adolescent suicides, homelessness, and rural financial and personal crises as the decade came to a close.

Colleagues of long standing encouraged me to "codify" these experiences and learnings in consultation during an exciting sweep of history and employment. There is an especially great dearth in the area of administration of consultation services. If consultants, consultees, teachers, and students are to learn from one another, they must work hard at communicating experiences, both in writing and verbally. It is hoped that the result of my efforts will be rewarding for the reader.

The modus operandi in preparation of this book is as broad as the potential audiences are varied. Since efficiency of effort is critical for all in the helping professions, and the opportunity for recording experiences is rare, it seems that one's concern should be more about setting them down and less about the style of writing. In fact, the text has been prepared with clarity as a high priority. Where I can encapsulate complex concepts, I do.

Like most consultants, I have had to apply and adapt for consultation purposes relevant lessons both from education and experience in the discipline. In social work, as in the other helping professions, this in consultation practice and teaching still leaves much to intuition. But I did have the benefit of having broad and rich experiences, not only in providing and promoting consultation in many settings, but also as a consumer from a variety of consultants and professions.

For those who are more "doers" than writers, just to begin writing is excruciatingly painful, not to mention the ongoing suffering accompanying the baring of one's self on paper. For me, this difficulty is probably associated in some way with earlier unpleasant bouts of case recording. Reviewing the references was helpful but also deadly in prolonging the delay of "D (dictation) Day." When the arrival of "D Day" became undeniable, I finally dismissed the urge for further reference searches and outlining and began the terrible task. The late Walter Prescott Webb, a great Texas historian, put it well when describing difficulties in getting started with the writing of his book *Texas Rangers* (1959, p. 6): At some stage the author must say, "No more research, I will not be lured by new material. I will write this damn thing now." And so I have.

USE OF THE BOOK

This book is written as an educational tool for students, practitioners, and teachers to help them in provision, use, and teaching of consultation. I hope also that it will encourage new and extended uses of consultation to improve mental health and related human service efforts in prevention, diagnostic, and support endeavors. Like other books on helping strategies, this can be used best when the methods it suggests are amply supplemented with discussion of experiences from practice. Each reader will, of course, approach the book in an individual way, according to her or his experience and current interests in the practice.

Experiences from which the text is patterned cover a considerable number of years. In addition, research for some sections of the book, such as the study of consultation practice in selected mental health centers and the brief survey of teaching the subject in schools of social work, occurred several years before the manuscript was submitted for publication. Although some of the data are not current, they are included because they have importance for the reader. There is a timeless quality about the learning we gain from certain experiences, such as consultation with public health nurses. These and other consultation examples presented have relevance for the struggle in the 1990s with design and delivery of services for large populations in crisis. Examples include those suffering from substance abuse, the homeless, and the untold numbers of victims devastated by collapse of the rural economy in many sections of the country.

Not all readers will be equally interested in all parts of the book. Although review of the entire book will provide maximum benefits, each of the three major parts is a complete unit in itself and can be read independently.

The "why," "what," "who," and "how" chapters lead to one on "the doing." Then a real-life example of consultation is offered. The processes described there, as well as in other parts of the book, are readily transferrable to numerous human service organizations and communities.

The example is of a group mental health consultation with public health nurses. In addition to the consultation content and method presented, many supervisors should find the description and case recordings in the appendix useful in group supervision. It must be understood, however, that although supervision and consultation have many similarities, they also have important differences.

Next, we study consultation services in eight community mental health centers in several parts of the country as well as the effects on these services of budget constraints and of staff views on educational preparation for consultation.

In the final part of the book, ethical issues in consultation are presented and recommendations are made about the extension of consultation services and about possible refinements for teaching the practice. This material will have meaning for interested students, for supervisory, consulting, community development, and administrative personnel, for a variety of direct service providers in mental health and other human services, and for faculty in social work and other helping professions.

Recognition of contributors has far greater meaning for me, I'm sure, than for those whose names are mentioned here. The list, incomplete as it is, includes persons who come easily to mind as colleagues and associates in mental health activities over the years in Texas, Missouri, and elsewhere.

I am indebted for their acquaintance, their ideas, and their support, even though many may not recall or know how they assisted with this book. Nevertheless, I want to thank them for helping enrich my professional life as well as helping me start and conclude this work. Sadly, it is too late to personally thank some persons, except through acknowledging precious memories of their lives and their gifts to me.

Special gratitude is expressed to:

- Fayette A. McKenzie, who introduced me to the profession of social work when I had the good fortune in college to serve as his student assistant in sociology;
- Ruth I. Knee, who was my first consultation supervisor while I was employed in a public health service mental health clinic for government employees;
- Virginia M. Satir, who provided strong encouragement to speak and write about consultation, and who would have contributed a chapter to this book had it not been for her untimely death in 1988;
- Charles F. Mitchell, director and long-time friend in Texas and Missouri, who stimulated and promoted innovative techniques of prevention and consultation;
- Michael J. Kelly, coordinator of the Social Work Extension Program at the University of Missouri–Columbia, and faculty colleague, who urged me to "codify" concepts, experiences, and teaching in social work/mental health consultation;
- Judith A. Davenport, whose penetrating critique of earlier versions of the manuscript was invaluable when she was on the faculty of the University of Georgia, as was her support of my expansion and completion of the book in her subsequent position as director of the School of Social Work, College of Human Environmental Sciences, University of Missouri– Columbia.
- I am also thankful to the many others who were the recipients (and the best "teachers") of my consultation efforts, and to the following for their acquaintance and inspiration:
- in Texas: Charlotte Bambino, Ellis Barham, Spencer Bayles, Paul Bolton, Sarah Conklin, Fred Crawford, Louis DeMoll, Waller Ethridge, Elizabeth Gentry, Guadalupe Gibson, Phoebe Hommel, Ira Iscoe, Charles Jaekle, Robert Ledbetter, Jerome Levy, Joseph Long, Brandoch Lovely, Wallace Mandell, Ray Metzger, Elvira Oetken, Alma Rollins, Glen Rollins, Dorothy Schultz, Bert Smith, Kelly Spratlan, Robert Sutherland, Ila Fern Warren, Wendell Williams;
- in Missouri: Paul Bowman, Judith Burke, Garnet Clark, Richard Cravens, James Currall, Leonard Douglas, Phyllis Ehrlich, Katherine Hill, Duane Kroeker, Barry Levin, James McNeal, Roland Meinert, Clara Louise Myers, Arthur Nebel, Frank Neff, George Nickolaus, Frank Paiva, Glenda Postle, Arthur Robbins, Fred Robinson, John Saunders, John Stretch, Paul Sundet, Katie Walker;
- nationally: Bertram Brown, Jeanette Chamberlain, Louis Cohen, Mary Gilmore, Margaret Hoffman, Victor Howery, Alberta Jacoby, Irving Jacoby, Blair Justice, Donald Klein, Therese LaLancette, Warren Lamson, Elizabeth McDonald, James Maddux, Vincent Mannino, Katherine

Oettinger, Jane Oltman, Dan Prosser, Lydia Rapaport, Milton Shore, Nathan Sloate, Morton Wagenfeld, Milton Wittman;
- to family: my wife, Emily, and our children, Janice, Michael, and Elizabeth, with great appreciation for their love and support during the many experiences essential to writing this book—experiences that at times infringed all too heavily on responsibilities as husband and father;
- and to son, Eliot, with loving memories of his affection, intelligence, and creativity, whose continued existence and contributions might have been realized if appropriate consultation had been available during critical periods of his short life.

Dwight Rieman

REFERENCE

Webb, W. P. (1959, January 24). Webb's recollection of boyhood on the plains. *Texas Observer*. Washington, D.C.: American Historical Association, pp. 6–7.

PART I

The Why, What, Who, and How of Social Work Consultation

CHAPTER 1

"The Why"
The Timeliness and Importance of Consultation

DOING MORE WITH LESS—MULTIPLIER EFFECTS OF CONSULTATION

The building and exchange of knowledge, always important, are critically needed now when mental health facilities and other human services agencies have to "do more/better with less." While social, emotional, and economic problems have mounted, supports for mental health and related services, particularly from federal sources, have been dramatically reduced.

Consultation, an essential service in years past, becomes even more critical under the "new federalism." Through the multiplier effects of consultation, small numbers of experts can radiate data and techniques to large numbers of caregivers, who in turn can help many people in need of preventive and supportive services.

The task of promoting and protecting the mental health of the population requires imaginative variation and enlargement of present methods. We must be concerned not only with those who are sick, but also with keeping well people well. It seems safe to assume that in the next decade there will not be enough mental health specialists to help even all of the sick, let alone the "well" people troubled with simpler, commonplace problems.

Consultation is an invaluable method for improving and extending preventive, remedial, and educational efforts for at-risk and other large populations. Looking at only one very vulnerable population, for example, it is modestly estimated that there are at least half a million cases of child abuse and neglect per year (*ADAMHA News,* 1980). Between 2,000 and 5,000 children are killed by their parents each year. Seven and one-half million children have serious emotional problems, and 80 percent of them are not getting help (Linkletter, 1989).

Table 1.1 presents mental health needs of the total population and the preventive approaches (including consultation) at primary, secondary, and tertiary levels through a variety of specialists, paraprofessionals, and other supportive individuals and groups.

Prominent among allies for mental health professionals, in provision of preventive and remedial services, are public welfare personnel. Although they are not usually labeled "mental health workers" and may not think of themselves in that role, certainly their functions can be supportive of mental health at any of the levels shown in the table. Through consultation, such welfare workers can improve their skills so they are able to help clientele maintain or restore mental health in the course of regular contact with them. These personnel may be in child protection, family therapy, income maintenance, or many other areas.

There are many opportunities in both public and private social agencies to do "mental health work," both as an individual worker and in alliance with other community care-givers. There are also numerous opportunities for welfare personnel, particularly in rural areas where they are highly visible, to assist with the orderly development and maintenance of mental health and related human services.

We must stretch our minds and actions in search of innovations and extensions in services for troubled people. We must struggle with decisions about how to accomplish the most with the fewest people and the least effort. Mental health professionals need allies to carry out large-scale preventive, education, and treatment activities. Consultation provided by mental health professionals can help to develop and extend the helping skills of allies.

Teachers, physicians, ministers, nurses, and others in daily contact with large numbers of people can provide preventive services and help with many of the emotional problems in the people they serve—often more easily and more effectively than mental health personnel because of existing relationships and ease of entry into problems. Consultation can teach allies how to apply mental health concepts and integrate them effectively in their daily work. Especially in their contacts with well people, particularly during periods of crisis, these allies can help protect them from prolonged or chronic disturbance.

Porterfield (1959) pointed out 30 years ago that influence of opinion leaders on the patterns of services in health, education, welfare, and recreation is well established, yet consultation and educational efforts aimed at "enlightenment" of such leaders have received little attention. What Porterfield said has as much relevance today as it did then:

> If it were possible to provide some kind of mental health training for the opinion leaders and caretakers, these key people might be able to do a more

TABLE 1.1. MENTAL HEALTH SERVICES: NEEDS, KINDS, GOALS, AND PROVIDERS (A PREVENTIVE APPROACH—TOTAL POPULATION: 250 MILLION)

	Primary Care	Secondary Care	Tertiary Care
NEEDS	85%, or about 212 million people	14%, or about 35 million people	Less than 1%, or about 2.5 million people
KINDS OF SERVICES	Education, information, anticipatory guidance, crisis support	Specialized clinical: diagnosis and treatment	Institutional and community care
GOALS	Promote wellness and keep people well	Early case finding and intervention. Remedial efforts. Reduce risk of more serious problems. Avoid chronicity. Work toward wellness and/or coping.	Reduce severity. Habilitation/rehabilitation
PROVIDERS OF SERVICES	Mental health and allied care-givers	Mental health and other care-givers	Mental health and other care-givers

Examples:

Clergymen
Nurses
Physicians
Public and private social workers
Teachers
Lawyers
Public housing staff
Pharmacists
Head Start and other indigenous workers
Morticians
Barbers
Beauticians
Bartenders
Relatives
Friends
Self-help groups
Mental health associations, PTA and other organizations
Well-being clinics

effective job. Ultimately they might create a kind of therapeutic environment in the community and spread a "contagion of health." In the long run such environments would tend to reduce the incidence of mental illness and permit the management and treatment of the less seriously ill in the community. (pp. 7–8)

(Additional information and rationale in support of mental health consultation are provided in Chapter 6, "A Study of Consultation Services in Eight Community Mental Health Centers.")

Unfortunately, there has been a marked decline of consultation and education services during the past decade and a shift away from the position of missionary-like zeal concerning these services (1960s and 1970s). Because the value of preventive activities could not be "proved," skepticism developed about the worth of consultation. In addition, budgetary constraints and inadequate educational preparation contributed to reduction of nonclinical services, even though they are needed now more than ever.

Within the past decade there has also been considerably less emphasis on work with the total population, and a narrower focus on the severely and chronically mentally ill. With this restricted focus has come renewed emphasis on traditional diagnostic, treatment, and rehabilitative services.

THE BUILDING AND EXCHANGE OF KNOWLEDGE

Consultation has emerged slowly and somewhat unevenly since the late 1940s. Compared with clinical and other direct helping services, it is a much newer and less well understood helping strategy. Although the number of references on consultation have increased considerably during the past few decades, it is still somewhat difficult to find good teaching materials for either students or practitioners. Particularly lacking are references on "the how," "the doing," and ethics. After giving some basic operational definitions and discussing consultation characteristics, this text will address these subjects. It will also detail examples from the field of consultation.

Further arguments in support of additional knowledge about (and education in) consultation are given in two studies. The first, a national study of selected mental health centers, revealed that consultation appeared to be the least understood of the essential services, in terms of both what it is supposed to consist of and what it is supposed to accomplish (Glasscote, Sussex, Cumming, & Smith, 1969).

In the second study (Cherniss & Egnatios, 1978), "Is There Job Satisfaction in Community Mental Health?" the authors report that a major source of frustration and work alienation for staff was being thrust into activities for which they had received poor training and supervision. One of these activities is consultation. The authors recommend that work satisfaction could be increased through staff development and good in-service training, especially in those areas where staff feel less confident (consultation and community organization). We begin our exploration in Chapter 2 with basic definitions and descriptions of the process of social work consultation.

REFERENCES

ADM facts heard at family conference. (1980, June 13). *ADAMHA News*, 6(12), 1–8.

Cherniss, C., & Egnatios, E. (1978, Winter). Is there job satisfaction in community mental health? *Community Mental Health Journal, 7*(4), 309–310.

Glasscote, R. B., Sussex, J., Cumming, E., & Smith, L. (1969). *Community mental health centers—Interim appraisal.* Washington, D.C.: Joint Information Service of The American Psychiatric Association and The National Association for Mental Health.

Linkletter, A. (1989, August 25). ABC Radio.

Porterfield, J. D. (1959, April). Community responsibility for mental health. *Public Health Reports, 74*(4), 303–308.

CHAPTER 2

"The What"
Consultation: Definitions, Distinctions, Types

SOME DEFINITIONS

Consultation is a method and process to:

1. enhance knowledge
2. improve skills — for providing better
3. modify attitudes — services to clients.
4. change behavior

A *consultant* is a change agent who brings special content or knowledge to change the consultee. The *consultee* may be an individual, group, organization, or community. The consultant serving as a facilitator, for example, might also use a process to produce change in work behavior.

Consultation is not "to do," but to help another to do. Galileo said, "You cannot teach anything to anyone—you can only help him to find it within himself." Also applicable is the following statement from an anonymous source on leadership: "A *good* leader inspires others to have confidence in *him*. A *great* leader inspires others to have confidence in *themselves*."

Consultation, furthermore, as we refer to it in this book, is not limited to client or consultee centered individual and group approaches, but includes administrative, program planning, and citizen and professional leader centered (community organization) types of consultation. It would include, for example, help with problem diagnosis, interventive methods, working with other caregivers in provision of services to vulnerable persons and their families (inter/

intra-agency cooperation), and organizing community services to fill gaps in existing human services.

DISTINCTIONS: CONSULTATION VERSUS SUPERVISION, ADMINISTRATION, CONTINUING EDUCATION

Consultation is similar in some respects to supervision in that it is a helping process, an educational process, and a growth process achieved through an interpersonal relationship. The kind and quality of relationship is the most significant factor in both cases. The worker's operations should not mirror the supervisor's or consultant's own method or philosophy.

A key aspect of consultation is that it is requested by the consultee and its use is entirely optional. Unlike the supervisee, the consultee is free to accept or reject the consultant's suggestions according to his or her own professional judgment and conscience.

Gorman (1963) states, ". . . no single variable characteristic can distinguish consultation from other social work activities. It is distinguished rather by a particular constellation of characteristics." Ideally the consultee has recognized a need for help, sometimes with the aid of the supervisor or administrator, and has asked for it. The consultant is a resource person called upon to provide what it is that other staff cannot provide.

The consultant is a specialist who does not carry administrative responsibility. He or she is not responsible for the basic orientation of the worker, or for the overall techniques or procedures in daily operations. Further, consultation is based on the authority of ideas, not on administrative authority, so the consultee may or may not accept these ideas.

Consultation is not a substitute for supervision or administration, although its services can be utilized most effectively if they are made available simultaneously to the administrator, supervisors, and staff. Supervisory and administrative understanding and acceptance of consultation will significantly influence the way consultation is used by the staff.

Consultation also is in many ways similar to staff development and continuing education, both growth-oriented activities as well. One important difference is that continuing education is usually more structured and has a predetermined "prospectus" and "agenda." It also often lasts longer than consultation, which may involve only a single contact or a series of limited contacts. Consultation may, in addition, put more burden on the consultee for problem solving or for choosing from alternative courses of action.

Maddux (1955) explains: "Teaching differs from consultation in that its goal is development of skill and knowledge, although it may utilize problem-solving methods. Consultation, on the other hand, emphasizes problem solving as the final goal, although there may be incidental growth in skill and knowledge."

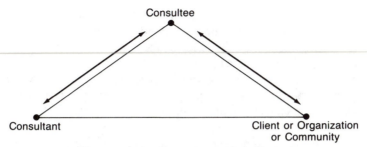

Figure 2.1. The Interactions in Consultation

One of the many special challenges in consultation is that the consultant must simultaneously (1) *learn* (gather data), (2) *feel* (what is going on with this individual or group), (3) *observe* (body language, group behavior, etc.), and (4) *give* (suggestions, questions, impressions, and alternatives). These requirements are especially demanding when the consultant is working with a group. Although the task is stressful, it can also provide professional excitement for the consultant, who must be comfortable in a risk-taking role.

In summary, to define consultation in the simplest terms: It is one person assisting another (or group) with work concerns—not personal problems. It can also be described as one person helping a second person around a third person's problems. Figure 2.1 illustrates this relationship.

There are many misconceptions with regard to consultation. It is an overused and sometimes abused term. Sometimes qualities of omniscience and omnipotence are attributed to the consultant. The process at times has become "cultish," with some viewing it as the answer to everything and the consultant seen as the all-competent, all-knowing "Big Doc in the white coat."

There is also opinion at the opposite extreme. As with other kinds of helping services, certain humor has evolved about consultants. One joke which made the rounds not long ago: "If you can't do it, teach it. If you can't teach it, be a consultant!"

TYPES OF CONSULTATION

There are many systems for classifying the various types of consultation. We will look at two perspectives and then present a categorization that will be the basis of discussions in this book.

Caplan (1963 and 1970) categorizes four fundamental types of consultation, summarized below:

1. *Client-centered case consultation.* The primary focus is on a specialized assessment of the mental health problems of the consultee's client and ways of solving them.

2. *Consultee-centered case consultation.* The primary focus is not on assessing the problems of the client, but rather on assessing and remedying the work difficulties of the consultee as manifested in the request for help with the client.
3. *Program-centered administrative consultation.* The consultant deals with the problems in designing or administering a program or with institutional policies relating to the prevention, control, and rehabilitation of mental disorders.
4. *Consultee-centered administrative consultation.* The focus is on helping an administrator or a staff group handle difficulties in the planning and implementation of programs. This type of consultation, unlike the others, may be carried out on a regular, continuing basis through scheduled discussions of current difficulties, rather than through a short series of ad hoc sessions in response to an emergent problem.

Ketterer (1981) offers a more extensive classification of consultation and education services:

1. *Case consultation.* Helping care-givers in other agencies to help their clients achieve treatment goals.
2. *Care-giver consultation and training.* Assisting professionals, paraprofessionals, and lay helpers to become more effective in their roles, as well as assisting them to develop ties to relevant professional agencies.
3. *Administrative consultation.* Providing technical expertise to community organizations and administrators regarding program design, management, evaluation, and organizational development.
4. *Program consultation.* Providing technical assistance to community agencies about the content of their programs.
5. *Grass-roots consultation.* Assisting informal community groups to identify needs, to develop methods for meeting needs, to seek resources, and to develop problem-solving strategies.
6. *Network/coalition-building.* Working in interagency or group coalitions to enhance community well-being, to share information and resources, and to address pressing social issues.
7. *Public mental health education.* Informing the community about services provided by the CMHC and other organizations; changing knowledge and attitudes about mental health through public presentations, literature dissemination, media, and the like.
8. *Competence training.* Providing in-depth training to normal and at-risk groups in order to increase their problem-solving skills and coping strategies.
9. *Community crisis intervention.* Intervening in community crises to reduce tension and identify underlying problems and issues.

For the sake of brevity and simplicity in this book, the following categorization is offered along with the purposes of each type:

Types of Consultation	*Purposes*
1. Client centered (covering both client and consultee)	1. Improve knowledge, skills, and attitudes in the delivery of services
2. Program-administrative (covering both administration and program)	2. Strengthen programs; enhance working relationships, both intra- and interagency
3. Citizen and professional leader centered (community organization)	3. Assist with planning and implementation of services
4. Consultant–consultant (consultee) centered	4. Develop/refine consultation methods

In other words, using mental health community organization consultation as an example, the consultant assists with the process but is not necessarily directly a part of it. It is the strategic persons in the community who do the actual organizational work from initial point of concern to establishment or extension of needed services. The consultant offers skilled help to care-giving and citizen leader personnel to assist them in the study and organizational tasks necessary to develop or extend services in the community.

REFERENCES

Caplan, G. (1963, April). Types of mental health consultation, *American Journal of Ortho-Psychiatry*, 470–481.

Caplan, G. (1970). *The theory and practice of mental health consultation*. New York: Basic Books.

Gorman, J. F. (1963) Some characteristics of consultation. In L. Rapoport (Ed.), *Consultation in social work practice* (chap. 2). New York: National Association of Social Workers.

Ketterer, R. (1981). *Consultation and education in mental health*. Beverly Hills, Calif.: Sage Publications.

Maddux, J. F. (1955). Consultation in public health. *American Journal of Public Health, 45*, 1424–1429.

CHAPTER 3

"The Who"
Sponsors and Consumers of Consultation: Settings and Services

Rapoport (1963) notes the rapid growth of consultation as an area of social work practice and its emergence in various ways in response to different needs. In *medical social work,* it was stimulated by the need for interdisciplinary collaboration in a multidiscipline setting and for teaching of allied disciplines. In *public welfare,* consultation grew from pressing needs for improving professional practice and skills and providing standards and control, with focus on in-service training and policy development in program planning. According to Rapoport, consultation is the most recent burgeoning development in the *mental health* field; it is an outgrowth of acute personnel shortages and the trend toward including indirect community mental health services as part of the direct service base and connecting such services with prevention of mental illness. Rapoport notes that consultation in the mental health field is linked with adapting clinical approaches to problem solving by non-psychiatric workers in the mental health aspects of their work.

Related to the core concern of this book—introduction, maintenance, and extension of consultation services (sponsor and consumer)—is the list given below of some types of organizations at federal, state, and local levels that provide and receive consultation services.

The most noteworthy example in the human services area at the *federal* level, with its regional components (until recently), is the health, education, and welfare complex.

At the *state* level, some of the major *public* organizations that offer and receive consultation services are these:

1. Departments of health
2. Departments of mental health
3. Departments of welfare
4. Departments of education
5. Departments of institutions
6. Youth authorities
7. Vocational rehabilitation agencies
8. Universities (through their extension services; adult education departments; and training centers in nursing, social work, sociology, psychology, and psychiatry)
9. Offices of mental health planning (either as independent organizations or as parts of any of the above organizations)

Voluntary organizations that operate on a statewide basis (often with a network of local offices) include the following:

1. Mental health associations
2. Public health associations
3. Welfare associations
4. Mental retardation associations
5. Associations concerned with chronic illness (such as tuberculosis, cancer, heart disease, cerebral palsy, and multiple sclerosis)
6. Foundations (in Texas, for example, the Hogg Foundation for Mental Health has long provided and encouraged a variety of consultation services, with major emphasis on community, school, and university sponsored mental health services)
7. Statewide, regional, and national professional organizations in psychiatry, psychology, nursing, and social work

At the *community* level are these examples of providers and users of consultation:

1. Community councils
2. Mental health outpatient and inpatient services
3. Family and children's agencies
4. Health departments
5. Welfare departments
6. Public and parochial schools
7. Public and private hospitals
8. Voluntary health organizations and the network of local chapters of statewide organizations as noted above

In addition, private practitioners of medicine, psychology, and social work may offer and receive consultation services, as may personnel in judicial, probation and parole, law enforcement services, and religious organizations.

Consultation philosophy, methods of implementation, and type and extent of practice at the several levels do, of course, vary tremendously. Also the purposes for giving and receiving consultation services are as different as the organizations themselves.

In general, however, the purposes might be grouped into these categories:

1. Setting standards and improving programs
2. Extending programs
3. Solving problems at administrative, program, staff, and client levels.
4. Lifting the level of professional skills and their application
5. Extending use of professional and nonprofessional skills to both troubled people and well people, as a way of maintaining physical and emotional health
6. Improving and extending community organization efforts
7. Evaluating program and staff effectiveness

Within this range of purposes, at each level there are diverse consultation methods and a greater or lesser amount of monetary and administrative contaminants that affect the "purity" of the consultation process. The term consultation, as was noted earlier, is too often used to cover a multitude of processes, manipulations, and exhortations that may pervert standard consultation theory and practice.

We have now reviewed the importance and timeliness of consultation, have developed a working framework and definition of consultative services, have listed some of the organizations that use or offer consultation, and have mentioned a few of the purposes and determinants that shape the consultation approach and method. The obvious question now is *how* can we introduce, utilize, and improve consultation services within the administrative houses in which we either live, are invited to enter, or intrude as "party crashers."

Perhaps this modern version of the old story about the grasshopper and the ant is in order here, addressed to the point of making theory and ideas practical.

The grasshopper, as in the old story, was concerned about how he was going to survive the coming winter. His friend the ant had a ready answer. He explained that the roach is a hearty insect who has no trouble in winter or summer and has managed to perpetuate his kind for millions of years. "Just change yourself into a roach," he advised. The grasshopper thought this was a fine suggestion. "I'll do it," he said. However, after a little thought he went back to the ant and asked, somewhat puzzled, "But how will I do it?" The ant replied, "Oh, that's *your* problem. I gave you the idea, now *you* will have to work out the details!"

Although at times it is tempting to stop just with ideas, I do want to help in the struggle about how to put them into practice. The next chapter, "The How," deals with the practical aspects.

REFERENCE

Rapoport, L. (Ed.). (1963). *Consultation in social work practice*. New York: National Association of Social Workers.

CHAPTER 4

"The How"
Entry and Operations,
Expectations, Maintenance

GETTING INVITED

Invitations for consultation come in many ways. Potential consultees first must be aware that an agency is available for consultation services. Since the consultees normally have the freedom whether or not to choose the service, they must have developed some positive feelings through other associations with the consultant and organization, such as by having collaborated on direct services to a client or worked cooperatively on a community task force. One of the best ways to "get invited" is through word of mouth from those who had a good experience with the particular person or organization.

A consultant's knowledge of organizational, program, or direct service problems can be used to encourage an invitation if the consultant organization conveys effectively to the potential consultee that it can offer something to remedy the problems. In other words, one does not need to sit back and wait for the invitation. Consultation can and sometimes should be "promoted," after careful market research is done on the needs for such services.

If consultation comes from within the organization, workers should be aware that it is available, know the conditions for using it, and understand its purposes. Under these less "pure" circumstances, the consultee may well feel some authoritative pressures other than just the "authority of ideas."

There is less preoccupation or concern these days about the need for consultation to be uncontaminated. One of the facts of life is that most of us, even though spending a large proportion of our time in consultation, must also engage in administrative and program activities which may complicate the consulting role.

What is most important is that we understand at any given time *what* we are doing and *why* in our various roles, and recognize that frequently the line between consultation and some other activity is very thin indeed. In our multiple roles we must always strive for sharpness in definition and try to isolate consultation principles from those of other helping processes.

Towle (1949), who made so many significant contributions in the development of consultation theory and practice (much of it, unfortunately, not well publicized), pointed out 40 years ago that consultation, even though desirable, could not always be offered on a take-it-or-leave-it basis. She said:

> Professional consultation in the context of an agency must be practiced with close reference to administrative hierarchy focused from top-down. This applies to case work consultation as well as program planning. Administrative attitudes about consultation travel down the lines; they permeate the agency. The administrator's whole hearted interest, his ambivalence, his anxiety, his resistance will be reflected throughout.

EVALUATING THE REQUEST FOR CONSULTATION

Three questions are of fundamental importance in evaluating the request for consultation:

1. Who is making it?
2. Why?
3. Why is the request being made at this particular time?

The initial steps in responding to a request for consultation services are crucial ones. It is necessary to consider not only the person making the request, but the consultee system and the system from which the consultant comes.

Particularly if there are indications that consultation may be ongoing, some tentative appraisal of the consultee system is of critical importance. For the consultation to be effective, a consultee system must have basic competency in its own disciplines, particularly at administrative and supervisory levels. A majority of the staff must have considerable interest in those aspects of their work that prompted the request for consultation. In the beginning consultation effort, such interest is especially important at administrative and supervisory levels. The following are some of the qualities that consultees should have to benefit most from the consultation process:

1. Competency
2. Psychological and emotional security
3. Humility

4. Interest in consultation, but not as a replacement for supervision/ administration
5. Willingness to freely divulge information *and* feelings about problems (feelings are "facts," too)
6. Healthy amount of "disequilibrium"—flexibility, openness
7. Willingness to blend with group if group consultation is employed
8. Ability to organize information about the problem and sort out essential elements for discussion
9. Willingness to share with supervisor information and conclusions from consultation sessions

Also to be taken into consideration is the staff's willingness to use material from the consultees' case loads and other work experiences. Use of such material, in contrast to didactic material such as in formalized education, is essential.

It is important to test out whether consultation can be carried out concurrently with administrative, supervisory, and staff personnel. It has been my experience that the early consultation effort, especially if the consultation relationship is to be a sustained one, should be devoted exclusively to work with administrative and supervisory staff. If there is not significant involvement at these levels, the consultation effort, no matter how good in relation to staff personnel, can be quietly sabotaged, for example, by a hostile and resistant supervisor.

On the other hand, if there is resistance within the staff group but supervisors and administrators are convinced of the value of consultation, such resistance can be handled in a positive way through normal supervisory and administrative channels. An example can be seen in the following statement made by a mental health nurse who evaluated a group consultation effort with public health nurses (see Appendix B):

> Although the staff experienced some disappointment with the beginning group meetings, they did not, however, ask for them to be terminated. One could suggest that despite their disappointment, they still had some feeling that perhaps in later sessions they would be more satisfied, or perhaps they did not have much freedom to choose whether to remain in or to terminate the conferences. It was apparent that the nursing administrator felt that this kind of conference was very worthwhile for her staff, and her interest and approval may have been a strong factor in the staff remaining in the conference.

UNDERSTANDING THE SETTING/SYSTEM

It is important to have as many exploratory contacts as necessary, not only to evaluate the request for consultation, but also to get some understanding of the structure and setting in which consultation would take place. This would include the organization's objectives, its methods of accomplishing those objectives, type and number of staff, working relationships and attitudes toward other organizations with whom contact is essential, and staff involvement in the decision to obtain consultation. Further, just as the consultant must understand these and other complicated factors, so the consultee system should be given some understanding of the philosophy and framework within which the consultant operates.

Haylett and Rapoport (1964, p. 334) point out that as the consultant must try to learn about the consultee organization and its "professional subcultures," simultaneously the consultees are looking him over, "their natural curiosity tempered by many unexpressed expectations and fears." These authors compare an organization into which a consultant is introduced to a family that experiences disequilibrium and stress. "Organizations, like families, have geneologies and traditions, goals and responsibilities" and also peer relationships analogous to sibling relationships. "Only if a fairly stable equilibrium prevails can its members function optimally as a harmonious whole. Therefore, in even the healthiest system, the introduction of a mental health consultant necessitates some realignment of forces and sometimes arouses disproportionate anxiety at all levels." The consultee system will experience less anxiety, however, if there has been a prior, positive experience with the consultant.

Haylett and Rapoport's comparison of organizations and families is also applicable to the consultant who is attached to an organization in which she or he has consultative responsibility. With this kind of combined consultee–consultant system, family-like difficulties, rivalries, relationships, strivings for status, and the like may be even more marked than when the consultant is from an outside organization. I am reminded of a woman at an agency within which she had consulting responsibilities but no administrative authority. She once spoke about a problem involving the agency administrator, a supervisor of a particular service, and the consultant. The consultant recognized that this problem, if it was to be resolved, had to be presented to the administrator, a male. The consultant, however, went to the supervisor, a female. The consultant explained to me, "You know, it's easier to go to Mama."

GETTING ACQUAINTED

As part of getting acquainted and becoming familiar with the setting process, it is helpful to have a workshop in which the consultant and consultee group work together. The workshop experience also serves as one means of determining whether ongoing consultation is needed or desired. Although the consultant in this phase may serve more as trainer than consultant, this role is important in helping to pave the way for use of a consultant later on. The workshop can provide the foundation of a sound working relationship between the consultee system and the consultant. Also, workshop experience in problem solving and opportunity to test out content and methods facilitate continued consultation sessions.

If the consultation is to be primarily client centered and if staff knowledge of behavior dynamics is limited, the workshop (whether provided by the consultant or some other special resource person) can be a means of presenting theoretical material which will enhance the later use of the consultation process. Likewise, if group consultation is to be the accepted method, some introductory experience in group dynamics theory and methods is helpful.

The exploratory process should also include attempts to establish working definitions of the problems for which help is sought, whether they are client, program, or administrator centered. Frequently, an important contribution of the consultant at this point is helping the administrator, supervisors, and others to define the problems, or at least to put problems into more precise terms. Definition sometimes escapes the consultee, either because they are too close to the problems or because of other reasons.

Caution should be exercised so that the role of the consultant is not too precisely defined at this early stage. Since consultation is dependent primarily upon a relationship process, it is difficult to set the consultant's role in a meaningful way before there is considerable opportunity for interaction with the consultee system. There will be need for repeated redefinitions and refinements of problems and role. The "contract" should be flexible enough to permit creative interaction and exchange between the consultee system and the consultant along the many stages of their work together.

This early exploratory process might be compared to the intake process in clinics and social agencies, where attention is given both to problem definition and to determination of who in the helping organization can be most useful. The consultant should be concerned with objective discussion and suggestions about which consultant-person might be most useful, either in the consultant's system or in some other system.

As part of the getting-acquainted process, whether in preparation for a workshop or ongoing consultation, the consultant will find it useful to (1) accompany workers on visits to clients, (2) sit in with supervisors and workers during individual or group supervisory sessions, and (3) observe other kinds of staff meetings. These observations are done, of course, only if workers and supervisors are comfortable with them and willing to have the consultant with them.

In addition, again with the full blessing of the consultee system, it is helpful for the consultant to attend meetings of the consultee system with other community or state agencies. However, it must be made clear, before such observations, that the consultant is doing this for his or her own learning-orientation and not to evaluate staff or agency performance (See Chapter 7, "Ethics in Consultation.)"

SELECTING THE CONSULTANT

Shortages of personnel, severe enough in the many specialized helping services, are even more acute with regard to qualified consultants. The label "consultant" is overworked and much abused, with almost as much variation in kinds, training, and equipment for the role as there are for those labeled "social worker."

Scarce though consultants may be, the consultee system usually does have some choice in selection. It is important to exercise this choice and search diligently to find the consultant who is most suited for the problem-solving, problem-defining tasks desired. Whether the task is client, consultee, program, administration, or community organization centered, there are specialists in that area, and quite a few consultants are skilled in more than one area. However, whether the specialist in a particular area is available in the community or state is another matter.

It is frequently impossible to find the right specialist at the right time. We must recognize, too, that *no* consultant is better than a poorly equipped one who, failing to understand the complexities of the consultee system, can really create havoc. The consultant who is sensitive not only to such complexities but also to her or his own limitations can be of assistance—even if the consultant is improperly equipped on some other counts—if both consultant and consultee frankly recognize the limitations and are willing to struggle and learn together.

The consultee system should also carefully consider whether the potential consultant, from whatever discipline, has working knowledge and respect for the agency and workers within it, both theoretically and from direct knowledge and observation of the agency at work. Since the effectiveness of consultation is dependent primarily on a relationship process, the relationship between consultants and consultee, collectively and individually, must be characterized by acceptance, mutual respect, and freedom to reveal the self.

Can the consultant operate as a peer in a coordinate working relationship? Can he or she accept the fact that there are many in other disciplines who can and must provide services to troubled people and that no one profession has an exclusive? Does the potential consultant recognize the need to look beyond a "sickness" orientation, or is his or her understanding of human behavior limited or disproportionately slanted toward illness and pathology without an accompanying desire to improve knowledge about normal people, their problems and ways of working with them?

Some of these requirements and "probe points" were dramatically pointed out in work with faculty members at a seminary, early in my experience as a consultant. One of the faculty members had previously been the chaplain at a state hospital where I had worked with him in some in-service training projects for clergymen. Because of the earlier working relationship and mutual respect, he could speak frankly about attitudes of other faculty members toward me, attitudes that hindered an effective consultation relationship with them. In essence, what he said, on behalf of these faculty members, was:

> You people in social work, psychology, and psychiatry are "whippersnappers." The church has been working with troubled people for many centuries. We feel that we too know a great deal about people and their troubles. We must admit, reluctantly, that the church no longer looks after the total person as it once did, and we must depend on your help. But we want to be very sure about you, who you are, and what you believe about human problems before you can consult with us or before we can make referrals with confidence to social agencies.

After becoming a "student" in a number of lectures and discussions at the seminary in a course entitled, "History of the Care of Souls," I found I was much better accepted as a consultant by the faculty group and also their students.

What characteristics should one look for in a consultant? Following are some guidelines for the prospective consultee.

1. Professional competency and experience in a human service field
2. Psychological and emotional security. Personal and professional maturity are more important than chronological age. Some are mature at 20; some are immature at 75!
3. Nonauthoritarian, flexible, open attitude
4. Humility in large measure—the strength, courage, and honesty to say "I don't know"
5. Lots of intestinal fortitude
6. Informal, relaxed, comfortable behavior with individuals and groups
7. Understanding and acceptance of the consultee and ability to convey this feeling
8. Willingness to make personal/professional interests subordinate to consultee's interests and needs
9. Skill in interviewing, both individual and group
10. Willingness to show appropriate emotion
11. Nonjudgmental, tolerant attitude
12. Moderate (healthy) amount of aggressiveness so as to intervene, for example, when a group is in trouble during the consultation process
13. Conciseness of thinking and expression—thinking well on one's feet
14. Articulateness
15. Ability to consolidate information quickly—learn, feel, observe, give
16. Good judgment and intuition

For more discussion about these and other attributes, see Chapter 6, "A Study of Consultation Services in Eight Community Mental Health Centers."

Many or all of the above attributes clearly are also desirable for those providing direct services to clients. There are some differences, however, from clinicians and other direct service personnel. The following are desirable traits specific to consultants.

1. Willingness to pioneer, experiment with ways of providing services. Consultation is still a very new "art," and much less is known about it than about the provision of direct services.
2. Broad perspectives and strong interest in preventive and interventive services and ways of extending services beyond traditional diagnosis and treatment
3. No need to be in "direct control" (as in therapy)
4. Ability to find satisfaction in helping others do the job
5. Strong community and program interests
6. Comfort in work with groups as well as individuals
7. Skills in group problem-solving
8. Skills in nondidactic teaching methods
9. Willingness to "gamble" and to move even with incomplete information
10. No need to have direct contact with the client problem

THE ROLE OF THE ADMINISTRATION

The *consultee sponsor* (consumer) must have an interest in consultation, be involved in the consultation process, and be willing to accept change and a certain amount of "disequilibrium" resulting from the consultation process. The consultation should not be used as a substitute for supervision or administration. The consultee sponsor should also be flexible enough to change program, supervision, and administration if such is indicated during or following the consultation process.

The *consultant's sponsor* should recognize individual differences and understand that there is no one "model" or "style" for consultation. As consultants do not come from the same mold, neither should they be expected to perform as if they did. Individual consultation specialties, interests, and skills should be encouraged.

The consultant should be allowed as much latitude and flexibility as possible to operate creatively within administrative and program boundaries. This includes time to develop and cultivate consultant–consultee relationships without administrative expectations of rapid, dramatic, or even very visible results. Until we have more precise instruments to measure consultation effectiveness, we must rely heavily on the subjective and collective judgment of administrator–consultant and consultee systems.

The administration should encourage improvisation according to the consultant's own particular background and skills, but always within the bounds of the consultant and consultee systems. The progressive jazz musician performs most creatively as an improviser—yet always does so within a structure and does not lose sight of the main theme. Similarly, the creative consultant needs freedom to improvise but must do so also within a structure and theme and maintain "the beat." He or she may solo, but still as a member of a combo. The consultant needs support and inspiration from the administrator–supervisor–colleague team in defining structure, staying within it, and continually searching for objectivity.

The consultant does need help in setting time limits and in recognizing impurities of composition and performance in relationships with the consultee system. Consultants, too, need supervision.

The consultant needs stimulation and sustenance not only from within the sponsor's system, but occasionally from without through conferences, consultation, in-service training, and exchange programs, in order to maintain and improve consulting skills and interests and avoid burnout.

CHOICE FACTORS: TRAINING, EXPERIENCE, TASKS

Each type of consultation brings with it specific prerequisites.

Client-centered case consultation requires those with special skills, training, and interest in diagnosis, casework, and therapy. Any of the helping professions, such as from the field of mental health, can be helpful with this kind of consultation.

Consultee-centered case consultation requires skill in helping the consultee use her- or himself creatively in relation to the particular problem. Unless the consultee system requires expertise in a particular discipline, with clinical competence not being of top importance, then any of the helping specialists may be appropriate.

Program consultation requires skills in helping the consultee and the consultee system use their skills and interests creatively to develop, modify, or extend programs. The type of discipline may be of secondary importance. Knowledge by discipline may be essential if consultation is concerned with certain technical problems such as research. To this the psychologist, historically, has made a major contribution, but social workers, psychiatrists, sociologists, and nurses have also been contributing in this area.

Consultee-centered administrative consultation requires, of course, administrative skills and experience, and this is more important, perhaps, than the discipline from which the consultant comes. Caplan (1963) emphasizes the importance for those who act as administrative consultants to seriously study administration and social science "to augment the traditional knowledge of their own profession." He also notes: ". . . few mental health consultants have as thorough knowledge of administrative problems as they have of the psychosocial complications of an individual client, and they must be careful to restrict their help to those factors in the administrative situation, such as the interpersonal and group dynamic aspects, concerning which they do have special competence."

SELECTING THE METHOD OF CONSULTATION

For economy and effectiveness of effort, both consultant and consultee must give careful thought early on to appropriate methods for initiating and carrying out consultation. Doing so is of special importance when consultation is to be ongoing (with staff development implications), and perhaps of less importance in crisis consultation situations.

In many instances, selection of the consultant will somewhat automatically include selection of method, since some consultants, because of personal and professional preference, may insist on, say, individual consultation with staff and supervisory and administrative personnel, or group consultation with all staff levels.

One method—group or individual—is not necessarily superior to another, but if an otherwise excellent consultant cannot operate effectively in group situations (and other consultants are not available), then even if group consultation would seem to be the most desirable method, the consultee system will need to make adaptations if the need for consultation is sufficiently urgent.

There are obviously many problems that do not lend themselves to group attention. Also, problems discussed in group situations frequently should be supplemented with individual consultation with administrator, supervisor or worker, or some combination.

When there is a choice between individual and group method, I have come to opt for the latter. The group provides stimulation, inspiration, and "teaching." In addition, consultees in a group do learn from one another and change attitudes as a result of group consideration. There is a richness in learning potential to which each of the consultees contributes; synergy develops. Also, learning that occurs for the consultee presenting the problem occurs also for many of the other participants.

Individual consultation does have advantages. The consultee may find it easier to express him- or herself. The problem brought for consultation may not be of interest or concern to other individuals on the staff. Some consultants are not comfortable in group situations but may have great skills in working with individual consultees. Individual consultation is, however, the most expensive method, since the time invested is focused on only one individual.

Group consultation *requires,* of course, that the consultant be comfortable, interested, and skilled in group methods. The consultant must also be able to distinguish, in theory and practice, the differences between group consultation and group therapy. Group consultation is focused on the professional problem, whereas group therapy is centered on the personal problem.

It is essential for group members to be willing to reveal and invest themselves in terms of feelings and attitudes, but the deliberate focus is on professional relationships, not personal ones. The consultant (especially if oriented toward group therapy) is frequently tempted to allow "drift" toward group therapy.

Although group therapy skills are certainly applicable to group consultation in some respects, there are special skills and training required for the group process. Such training is also extremely valuable for improving effectiveness in all kinds of group situations requiring understanding of individual behavior in the group, total group behavior, and the requirements for productive group experience.

"Normal" amounts of stress—interpersonal relationship difficulties among staff, communication impediments, and the like, which exist to some extent in all organizations—can be alleviated particularly well when group methods are employed. Even though assistance with such difficulties is not necessarily a primary objective, promotion of an overall emotionally improved administration –supervisor–staff relationship and a decrease of emotional types of problems which block effective practices frequently come as an important by-product.

UNREALISTIC EXPECTATIONS: "BUT I CAN DREAM, CAN'T I?"

All parties may at times approach the consultation process with overblown expectations.

When a *consultee* fantasizes, he or she may imagine that consultation will:

- Make up for deficiencies in training or experience (Consultation cannot be a substitute for training or experience; it can only supplement these.)
- Replace the need for supervision/administration (This fantasy may result from certain problems in handling or using authority in a positive way.)
- Provide direct answers
- Solve problems
- Tell me "how to do it"
- Eliminate inter- and intragroup tensions and difficulties

When a *consultant* fantasizes, the expectations may be equally unrealistic. He or she might expect the consultee and organization to:

- Be totally involved and ready for consultation and free from concern about its impact
- Be receptive to and supportive of needed changes
- Be entirely clear about the consultant's role and function

- Be entirely open and frank in describing problems and his or her feelings about them
- Have problems well organized, defined, and concisely presented
- Be fully understanding and supportive of the consultant's methods, approaches, priorities, and so on

It is natural for both consultee and consultant to have and to enjoy their fantasies, but the sooner they both can understand what is unreal and what is real in their work relationship, the more effective it will be.

CARE AND FEEDING OF THE CONSULTANT–CONSULTEE SYSTEM

Personnel shortages, acute in all of the helping professions, are even more so in the "helper for the helpers" category. Unless proper safeguards are maintained, the consultant species is in danger, like the whooping crane of becoming extinct. If consultants are to survive, both sponsor and consumer systems must give serious thought to their "care and feeding." Following are ways in which the consultee system can take responsibility.

1. Keep the consultant informed about the consultee system and significant changes within it—staff composition, functioning, program objectives, relationship with other organizations, all other matters. Honest and frank exchange of information is essential if consultant and consultee are to perform effectively. It is never a good idea to put on a façade for the consultant's benefit.

2. Prepare for the consultant's visits and give some thought to how best to utilize the time together. The consultant's time is limited too. Try to schedule appropriate amounts of time for the several consultant functions. If a particular function is completed in less time, the consultee should help the consultant to know the need has been met.

3. If emergencies occur within the consultee system that would prevent effective consultant–consultee interaction, reschedule the consultation visit if possible. Some emergencies or crises, however, can sometimes be most fruitful for consultation when the "iron is hot."

4. Consider whether the problems are best for discussion with the consultant. Have resources within the consultee system been appropriately explored? Is the timing sequence for discussion right?

5. Provide enough information about the problem so the consultant can understand it, its duration, its severity, and why it was selected for discussion at this time. Also, what kind of help from the consultant is desired? Don't be coy. Most consultants are not clairvoyant!

6. In addition to giving necessary briefing during consultation conferences, fill the consultant in on significant developments or problems between visits. Share pertinent copies of correspondence and other written materials, provided they don't violate confidentiality within the system. Running off an extra copy requires little effort and expense, and yet its value may be considerable. It is always much better to overinform than underinform the consultant.

7. If possible, set aside work matters or problems that are not related to the consultation need. Distractions prevent effective penetration of the problem for both consultee and consultant.

8. Conceptualize: What seems to be the core problem, and what are the essential details? Don't clutter up the interaction with extraneous information or blow-by-blow descriptions that are not central to problem solving. But don't kill spontaneity of expression either—about feeling or fact!

9. Keep some notes (consultee and consultant) of what was discussed in previous consultation sessions, what was and was not solved, what needs attention now. If the same problem was discussed before, are these new phases of the core problem, or is the consultee still fixated on the same issues—and if so, why? The consultee has some responsibility for isolating the problems for discussion and resolution.

10. Arrange suitable conference settings and privacy when necessary. If the consultee condones interruptions, distractions, or "fish bowl" settings which detract from effective discussion, both consultant and consultee share the responsibility for finding the reason. Is it, for example, a way of avoiding or wishing to discontinue consultation?

11. Don't use the consultant to manipulate people or situations, especially when such use is unrelated to the problems for which consultation is sought.

12. Remember that the consultant is human, with human frailties, needs, and problems that cannot always be submerged or handled in the most professional manner. The consultant experiences some of the same kinds of "loneliness" the administrator feels. He or she is removed from the satisfaction of direct service. Often results of consultation efforts are not visible or the consultant does not get feedback via the consultee.

Maddux (1955, p. 1425), on the problem of work gratification, says of the consultant:

> He is not ordinarily permitted to perform the task for which he was trained; he is required to help someone else do the job. His gratification must come, at least in part, from seeing someone else succeed; and he needs the endurance to permit another to fail at a job in which he thinks he could have succeeded. The consultant's frustration in this area sometimes prompts him to take over and attempt to do the job for the consultee.

13. Let the consultant know your thinking about how consultation services might be improved and, more specifically, what both consultant and consultee might do to improve the working relationship and effectiveness.

14. Let the consultant know if he or she is "getting through." What is helpful? What is not helpful? I recall from a consultation experience some years ago my frustration in this regard with a consultee who apparently absorbed and utilized much from our work together but, sphinx-like, revealed none of this. The only way I knew I was bringing something of importance to the consultee was from materials he prepared for speeches and other purposes, in which there were numerous references from our discussions and from material I had prepared.

15. Let the consultant's own sponsor system know occasionally what benefits are coming from the consultation experience. Such communication need not wait until consultation is concluded or discontinued.

16. Consultants, like consultees, appreciate opportunities for social interaction and even enjoy one another's company outside of the work situation. However, social interchange should be somewhat selective. Especially if consultation is prolonged, consultant and consultee need to get away from each other and avoid "neurotic dependency." Each should respect the other's "no" to social invitations and encourage freedom of choice. The consultant is usually resourceful about taxis, hotel accommodations, travel schedules, and the like. If assistance is needed with such matters, the consultant should make this fact known. The consultation relationship should not be cluttered up with these trivia, nor should social occasions be cluttered with problems that are more appropriately discussed during sessions scheduled for this purpose.

THE CONTRACT—STATEMENT OF UNDERSTANDING

A succinct description of contract is simply: "an exchange of promises" (Pittman, circa 1954). A dictionary definition emphasizes legal implications: an agreement between two or more parties, usually written and enforceable by law. In human services usage, the first association with the term "contract" is a legal one. This is understandable but unfortunate, because it may restrict discussion and agreement on conditions surrounding the consultee–consultant relationship.

Although the term "contract" is borrowed from law and business, it can be usefully applied to mental health and other human services for outlining the ground rules for worker–client, worker–family, worker–group, and other relationships. Usually the contract in these circumstances is not a legally binding one, and therefore, unlike legal contracts, it offers flexibility for renegotiation

(Seabury, 1987). When problems arise in consultation delivery, it is important to review contract provisions and make changes in work arrangements as needed.

I have found it useful to refer to the agreement as a "Memo/Statement of Understanding." This term avoids preoccupation with negative legal associations which may inhibit concurrence about the work relationship.

A statement of understanding should be concluded only after a thoughtful period of exploration by both consultee and consultant. "Atmosphere" and "ingredients" for such exploration, along with essential ethical considerations, are presented in Chapter 7, "Ethics in Consultation."

Fees, time requirements, and similar matters should be considered only after careful exploration has answered the basic question of whether there is a proper fit in the consultant–consultee relationship. Once a satisfactory fit is determined, then such conditions and other requirements for both parties will be easier to outline.

If there has been thoughtful and satisfactory exploration, a written agreement may not be essential, particularly where time is limited. However, even in short-term arrangements, there are good arguments for putting a contract in writing. Caplan (1970, p. 65) advises: "The written word is an excellent way of revealing misunderstandings, which may be obscured in verbal discussions. It is important that these be corrected as early as possible in order to arrive at true consensus."

The statement of understanding need not be elaborate and should be fairly easy to complete once basic mutual trust and respect are assured. Rather than a highly formal and legalistic document, I favor a "psychological" agreement that gets at the essence of what is expected of each party and that makes explicit what is necessary for an effective alliance. Boss (1986) outlines an excellent series of questions for the exploratory contact, diagnosis of organizational difficulties, problems for resolution in the contracting session, and some strengths of a psychological contract that clarifies goals of consultation.

Since audiences, climate, circumstances, and purposes of consultation vary tremendously, it is difficult to present here every item that should be covered in a contract/statement of understanding. However, whether the consultee is an individual, group, organization, community, or segment thereof, general categories for inclusion are the following:

1. Who are the parties responsible for the initial statement of understanding and any later revisions
2. Brief statement of the problem for which consultation is sought, how long it has existed, and reasons for intervention now
3. Audience—with whom will the consultant work
4. Goal—what is supposed to happen as a result of the consultation process
5. Ground rules and responsibilities of consultee and consultant, both individual and shared
6. Fee

The *ground rules and responsibilities* should be made fairly explicit. The following items are suggested:

- Time—span, and projected total and amount of time per session
- Method—individual, group, use of "live" case materials, intra- and interagency conferences, and so on
- Support services—recording, reports, conference space and accommodations, scheduling, and so on
- Confidentiality—what cannot be shared, what can be shared and with whom, flexibility in certain circumstances (See Chapter 7, "Ethics in Consultation.")
- Discussion content—cases, simulations, references, individual and joint responsibilities
- Evaluation—methods, staffing, timing, reporting, and so on
- Systematic review and renegotiation of agreement
- Termination—circumstances, timing, preparation, and reporting

The content of the statement of understanding and the process utilized in its completion are of course early and crucial steps which can either negate or lay a solid foundation for a successful consultation experience. To help ensure an effective beginning relationship also, it is beneficial to involve all potential consultees in planning the consultation project, developing the general items in the statement of understanding, and revising as needed during the life of the project. This may not be possible in all circumstances, but it should be at least considered by the responsible parties.

Ideally, all participation in planning and execution of the project should be on a voluntary basis. There are circumstances, however, when even reluctant potential candidates should be actively encouraged or even required to participate in group sessions of the project. Examples are given in Chapter 5. In the case described there, the commitment of the nursing administrator to the project, her active participation in it, and administrative pressure from her upon all her staff resulted in successful involvement of nearly all those who were initially resistant to the project.

Another factor that will help ensure success and should be a part of the contract statement is repetition with participants concerning the background and purpose of consultation. This may be done as a matter of routine, or when participants ask directly or through inference, "Why are we here?" Stresses in the process make such reinterpretation especially important, both for those who have been involved for some time and those who are just entering the relationship. I have found that orientation and reorientation are particularly effective if participants at all levels are encouraged to be active in the procedure, with the consultant remaining in the background, acting mostly in a supportive or clarifying role.

Fees is another area that deserves specific attention. It is often one of the first items considered by the consultee, and it might also be the item of highest priority for a consultant considering an invitation for assistance. Fees for consultation vary widely because of the vast range of differences in consultee–consumers, their circumstances, and the disciplines required for consultation services. Other factors affecting fee are the demands for service, complexity and volume of the problems, and availability of appropriate competent consultants.

Variation in fee charges also occurs because "consultancy has made minimal effort to formally standardize or publicize fee schedules" (Payne & Desman, 1987, p. 109). Currently the field is pretty much a consultants' market, grounded on what the market will support. Consultants from business, medicine, and law probably command the highest fees. Mental health and other disciplines from the human services are paid less well, with social work often at the lower end of the range.

I believe that all too often fees are exorbitant. Reasonable guidelines for reimbursement, framed according to task complexities and consultants' ability to meet them, are rare. Attention to ethical implications of fee practices is urgently needed for all consulting professions. A gross example of apparent disregard for such ethics is given by Waas (1989, p. 66). He describes a "consulting fee" charged by Frederick Bush (no relation, but President Bush's top political fund raiser for many years) for a HUD rehab project in Puerto Rico. He never visited the site. His fee was $160,000!

References on the subject of fees are few, and cautious, as they are in the whole broad area of ethics in consultation practice. Although eminent educator and ethicist Roger Heyns is encouraged "by evidence of a newfound American willingness to consider ethical issues" (Kidder, 1989, p. 12), the field of consultation has not kept pace with public interest in ethical concerns, if the sparse literature and inadequate codes are gauges of progress.

The NASW Code of Ethics, for example, though an important "symbolic document" for the practitioner, provides little guidance for the consultant concerning ethical decisions, including fees. The code states (1980, p. 954): "When setting fees, the social worker should ensure that they are fair, reasonable, considerate, and commensurate with the service performed and with due regard for the clients' ability to pay." Guidelines are needed to define what is fair, considerate, and commensurate with services performed.

Social work and other professions should pursue serious study on guidelines for fees and consistent application in consultation. Because of the complexities involved in consultation practice, standardization is more difficult than in clinical services, but there are certainly learnings from that area that can be adapted to make consultation fees more uniform and ethical.

A few references and suggestions are offered for some tentative and incomplete guides. Chenault (1986, p. 230), discussing internal and external sources of consultation, says "external consulting fees which are as high as $250 an hour may motivate top managers of moderate-profit companies to reexamine their consulting needs." Zasloff (1988, p. 240) using as an example the fees of consulting firms that arrange EAP services, suggests "an hourly fee which normally corresponds to the cost of a counseling session, $60–$90 an hour, whenever employees utilize this benefit."

For direction concerning fees for consultation, inquiry should be made from responsible sources in the professional community. In social work this might include committees of the local NASW chapter, schools of social work, community health and welfare councils, mental health centers, and the like. Prevailing rates for direct clinical services can be used as one guideline, if it is taken into account that consultation may require considerably more planning and reporting than is used in traditional practice. Also, since consultation is often provided on a regional, statewide, national, or international basis, travel and per diem expenses should be a part of the fee but listed as separate items.

Consultant and consultee should consider that consultation conferences are often less easily arranged on a sequential or hourly basis than are clinical sessions and therefore some financial adjustment should be made to compensate for this fact.

Special payment arrangements for consultation services, as recommended by the NASW code for direct services, are certainly appropriate when the consultee (individual, agency, or community) presents clear evidence of inability to pay a full fee, or even any fee at all. Corey, Corey, and Callanan (1988, p. 278) recommend that "Consultants donate time to agencies that are unable to pay."

To help ensure commitment on the part of both consultee and consultant to elements of the agreement, and to enhance psychological "bonding," both parties should participate in the preparation of the document, if it is a written one. Many consultees may be unfamiliar with the format of such agreements, so the consultant may have to assume primary responsibility for ensuring that essential elements are listed and for making suggestions about what items each party should draft.

Suggested categories appropriate for the consultee to draft include identification of the principal parties to the agreement, statement of the problem, consultation audience, and goals. The consultant might have primary responsibility for drafting (in cooperation with the consultee) items on ground rules (shared and individual responsibilities), support services, and fees. To some, this division of responsibility may seem like an unnecessary "chore." However, although having the consultant alone do it might save a little time in the beginning, it runs the risk of a flawed agreement and extra expenditures of time and effort later on.

REFERENCES

Boss, R. (1986). The psychological contract: A key to effective organization development consultation. *Consultation, 4,* 284–304.

Caplan, G. (1963, April). Types of mental health consultation. *American Journal of Ortho-Psychiatry, xxxiii*(3), 470–481.

Caplan, G. (1970). Building relationships with a consultee institution. In G. Caplan, *The theory and practice of mental health consultation.* New York: Basic Books.

Chenault, J. (1986). Decentralized internal consulting, *Consultant Education* (special issue of *Consultation*), *5,* 229–238.

Code of Ethics of the National Association of Social Workers, *Encyclopedia of Social Work* (Vol. 2).

Corey, B., Corey, M., & Callanan, P. (1988). *Issues and ethics in the helping professions* (3rd ed.). Pacific Grove, Calif.: Brooks/Cole.

Haylett, C. H., & Rapoport, L. (1964). Mental health consultation. In L. Bellok (Ed.), *Handbook of community psychiatry.* New York: Grune & Stratton.

Kidder, R. (1989, June 30). Avoid simple answer for complexity, *The Christian Science Monitor,* p. 12.

Maddux, J. F. (1955). Consultation in public health, *American Journal of Public Health, 45,* 1424–1429.

Payne, S., & Desman, R. (1987). The academician as a consultant. In S. Payne & B. Charnov, *Ethical dilemmas for academic professionals.* Springfield, Ill.: Charles C Thomas.

Pittman, W. (circa 1954). From a lecture at University of Missouri-Columbia School of Law. Notes courtesy of George F. Nickolaus.

Seabury, B. (1987). Contracting and engagement in direct practice, *Encyclopedia of social work* (Vol. 1). Silver Spring, Md.: National Association of Social Workers.

Towle, C. (1949). *Consultation.* Unpublished paper, University of Chicago School of Social Service Administration.

Waas, M. (1989, September). The sum of their possessions, *Harpers Magazine,* p. 66.

Zasloff, M. (1988). A corporate perspective on employee assistance consultants, *Consultation, 7,* 235–243.

PART II

"The Doing": Selected Examples from the Mental Health Field

CHAPTER 5

Group Mental Health Consultation with Public Health Nurses

The consultation described in this chapter is an outgrowth of the belief that social work knowledge and skill have a place in preventive activities in mental health. It rests on the assumption that non-mental health personnel, who are in contact with large numbers of people daily, need assistance in developing and extending their understanding and application of mental health principles. Consultation can strengthen their understanding of human behavior and of the helping relationship generally.

As was explained in Chapter 2, "The What," consultation is a helping, educational, and growth process achieved through an interpersonal relationship. It is based on authority of ideas, and the consultee is free to accept or reject the suggestions, according to his or her professional judgment and conscience. Unlike a supervisor, a consultant does not carry administrative responsibility. Ideally, the consultee has recognized his or her need for help, sometimes with the aid of the supervisor or administrator. The consultant is a resource person called upon to provide that "something" which the supervisor and local staff cannot provide.

This consultation work was done with public health nurses. The consultation service was administered by a state health department, division of mental health, with responsibility for developing community mental health services through such methods as in-service training, consultation, and initiation and appraisal of demonstration projects, with particular emphasis on prevention.

"Group Mental Health Consultation with Public Health Nurses," by Dwight W. Rieman, which appeared in Lydia Rapoport, ed., *Consultation in Social Work Practice*, National Association of Social Workers, Inc., copyright 1963. Adapted with permission.

A significant part of the activity was devoted to consultation with professional groups to strengthen the application of mental health concepts in their work. Because of the strategic position of the public health nurse, both in numbers of people served and in accessibility to people during critical life experiences, considerable time was devoted to work with this group in local health departments. The assumption was that the nurse is in a position to maintain and strengthen the mental health of patients and families.

Some services the public health nurse performs in which mental health skills are significant are as follows: (1) interviewing for identification or clarification of a problem, (2) establishing a supportive relationship with the patient, (3) motivating the patient to seek medical attention, (4) helping the patient to accept the diagnosis, (5) helping the patient to accept responsibility for following through on medical recommendations, and (6) educational activities, such as teaching health procedures to patients, holding health discussions with patients in groups or classes, and teaching in staff development programs for public health nurses.

The request for consultation from this local health department and its nursing staff was viewed positively by the Division of Mental Health and accepted because the philosophy of operations relating to the mental health components of nurses' work was generally consistent with the Division's objectives as described above. The nursing director's motivation for consultation at this particular time was also influenced somewhat by staff tensions and her desire to improve working relationships within the organization and with other community agencies. Some of her views on mental health applications in public health nursing and her interests in having consultation for her staff are presented in more detail later in this chapter, as well as in Chapter 7, "Ethics in Consultation."

The work to be described here was primarily a group consultation effort, but others might think of it as in-service training. It is considered consultation because of:

1. The nature of the relationship between consultant and consultee
2. The intensity of the effort
3. Use of participants' case materials for learning
4. The largely nondidactic teaching methods
5. The regularly scheduled, ongoing work, which continued for more than three years of monthly group discussions

BACKGROUND

The work was carried out with a public health nursing staff in a Texas city of approximately 350,000 population, which had experienced rapid growth in the past several decades and had become increasingly industrialized. There was a good basic framework of health, welfare, education, and recreation services, with great variation in the quality of professional services, however.

One public health department served the city while another served the county. The staff consisted of twenty nurses and five supervisors, plus several vocational nurses and student nurses who also participated in the consultation sessions. Also participating in many of the sessions was a nursing instructor from a local nursing school who had been on the supervisory staff when consultation began. The nursing program offered bedside nursing, maternity service, health supervision for infants and preschool children, clinic and follow-up care of tuberculosis patients, communicable disease control, venereal disease control, crippled children's services, and inspection and consultation services for maternity and child care centers.

The following excerpts are taken from written materials prepared by the nursing director and abstracted from the consultant's numerous discussions with her. They are indicative of (1) the mental health components of public health nursing as she viewed them, and (2) some of her motivation for use of mental health consultation.

- The public health nurse works with individuals and families in the home, clinic, school, and office. Her function as a member of the health team is to aid in prevention of disease, promotion of health, and prolongation of life.
- Much of her work is counseling any or all members of the family. Because health/mental health are related to the total productivity and well-being of the individual, the counseling encompasses many areas. It may include discussing the arrival of a new infant as a family member with a mother who is pregnant for the first time, or with a mother who has many children but who is anxious because of possible jealousies that might develop. It might be with a sick mother too concerned about a teenager flunking in school to seek medical care. It might be with an incapacitated "oldster" who lives alone and will not enter a care home. It might be with a person who cannot accept a diagnosis or seek medical care or remain under medical care. It might be with parents who cannot accept the necessity for having their children immunized against communicable diseases. It might be counseling with a representative of another agency that is working with a family in the nurse's case load or that might be accepting a referral. It might be discussion with a clinic physician or a private physician about a patient's family situation.
- Since counseling is on a face-to-face basis, a criterion of the ability to practice public health nursing is the ability to develop positive interpersonal relations.
- The question, "How well does this nurse get along with co-workers and patients?" is almost always asked by employers and others who work with nurses. When asked by the discerning person, it does not have to do

primarily with the social attributes of the nurse, although there may be some relationship. It does have to do with how well the nurse works with other staff nurses, supervisors, families and patients, and other professionals or agency people. It also has to do with whether she can accept supervision and whether she is a democratic, helping person or an autocratic, directive person. Can she be friendly without being familiar? Can she be accepting and understanding rather than judgmental? How does she handle her hostilities and prejudices? All these questions have to do with the nurse's emotions, personality, and mental health as these affect her ability to practice public health nursing.

- In nursing practice, "getting along with other people" is not restricted to nurse–patient or nurse–family relationships, nor limited to the hours of eight to five, Monday through Friday. It has to do with nurse–supervisor, nurse–administrator, supervisor–supervisor relationships, as well as nurse–community relationships. It has to do with the attitudes and feelings about people that are part and parcel of an individual personality. A nurse must like people. She must have some understanding of human behavior and the needs and drives that cause behavior. She must accept the fact that she never ceases to be a human being, a member of a family and community, when she is practicing nursing. She must know herself. She must have some understanding of her own prejudices, likes, and dislikes and be able to handle them so that she can use her skills in the best possible way in her work with people.

- Mental health, like physical health, is never static. One way of attempting to maintain good mental health, hence good interpersonal relations, is to participate in a mental health consultation program. This is not a therapy program, but a helping program where nurses meet with a mental health consultant to maintain and improve their professional skills. Although the need for maintenance may change from time to time, maintaining and developing skills are the reason why, as in any preventive program, consultation must be continuously available. Mental health consultation allows one to look at one's attitudes in relation to day-to-day work. We have used the case conference method. This looking at one's self is very trying. We are not always pleased with ourselves.

- The success of any project depends on good administration, which, in turn, depends on how well the administrator works with people. For this reason, what is said here is extremely personal in nature. Background material, or the "why mental health consultation" material, is necessary in order to be able to understand how the program was planned and executed and what the results were. One of my early concerns was how the staff and I could plan and execute a good public health nursing program. I was so disturbed about intrastaff tension and rivalry. As a new administrator I was not immediately accepted by the staff, so working together was extremely difficult for a long time. I wanted to provide a truly democratic

atmosphere so that everyone could realize her potential as a professional person and give good service to the community.
- As an administrator, I wanted to be warm, enthusiastic, stimulating. I wanted to be helpful without being authoritarian, firm without being rigid. I wanted to be comfortable as a leader. My conferences with the mental health consultant helped me to see the need for looking at myself in relation to being an administrator. This came hard.

PREPARATORY PHASE

Before the consultation sessions began, there were three two-and-a-half-day workshops which offered foundation material on such topics as principles of human behavior and interviewing relationships and methods. The first workshop was requested by the nursing director, who was motivated by concerns about nurse–patient relationships and also intrastaff relationships. The second and third workshops grew out of interests expressed by the total staff.

Before the first workshop, the consultant spent several days with the nursing staff for an orientation to their program. This included observations in child health conferences, home visits, and visits to community agencies with which the nurses worked frequently.

In addition to the presentation and discussion of basic content on human behavior and interviewing in the workshops, there was group discussion of "live" case material from the staff nurses' own practice. Group problem-solving methods were employed with two related goals: to develop new insights into a particular problem and more effective ways of dealing with it, and to encourage the application of this learning to patients and families with whom the nurses worked. At strategic points in the workshops, role-playing was used to supplement the discussion.

Each workshop was evaluated through written questionnaires and group discussion. This evaluation helped to determine the content and method of subsequent workshops. After the third workshop, the staff requested that the consultant provide ongoing consultation services.

OBJECTIVES OF CONSULTATION

Objectives were developed in pre–workshop discussions with staff, post–workshop discussions, and refined as needed at strategic points during the ongoing process with consultees. In summary they were to assist in:

1. Developing attitudes and skills that would help the nurses establish positive relationships with all patients
2. Developing the understanding that would enable the nurse to work with

whatever emotional problems were preventing the patient's effective use of the nurse's service

3. Applying mental health principles in all areas of public health nursing, with nonproblematic cases as well as problem cases, and with interpersonal relationships with staff and related agency personnel.

4. Promoting an overall emotionally healthy administrative–supervisory–staff relationship, and dealing with particular problems of an emotional nature which block effective nurse–supervisory or administrative practice.

5. Promoting understanding of other community agency activities and the importance of interdependence of action and pooled efforts toward meeting patient and family needs.

GROUP SESSIONS WITH STAFF NURSES

Group consultation sessions with staff nurses were held in two groups of about fifteen each. There were 28 monthly two-hour sessions. Twenty-one group sessions were also held with the supervisory staff. In addition, during each monthly visit the consultant conferred individually with the nursing administrator. The administrator and supervisors also participated in the sessions with the staff nurses. The consultant was available for individual conferences with staff and supervisors.

Content

The content of the sessions was centered on difficulties the nurses were having in their working relationships with patients and families. Specific concerns were illness, particularly chronic illness such as tuberculosis and physically or emotionally crippling conditions, unemployment, housing, and sanitation. Other topics were physical and emotional development of children, parent–child relationships; school adjustment, mental illness of a family member, interviewing attitudes and methods, assisting the patient to seek medical attention, and helping the patient accept the diagnosis and follow through on medical recommendations. Occasionally there were more didactic discussions on general topics such as delinquency, unmarried mothers, the aged, and adolescents. The purpose of these was to provide some theoretical material about human behavior as a means of sharpening insights into subsequent case material.

Considerable attention was also given to interagency cooperation and how the nurses might best work with other agency personnel. Occasionally, representatives from other health and welfare agencies were invited to participate in the discussions, particularly those involving some question of "who does what and why" and how a "team" of representatives from several community agencies might work together.

Discussion time was also devoted to the nurses' attitudes toward patients and how these affect working relationships. Case examples were used to present the patients as total persons and to generate more refined methods of working with them.

Method

Case material for group discussion was usually selected in advance. As a rule, the case was first discussed with the supervisor to determine whether it was appropriate and whether additional assistance or suggestions might be needed. The method of summarizing case material and the manner of presentation underwent considerable change as the result of their working together. After some experience, the consultant, along with the staff, prepared the following simple guide for the preparation of case material for group discussion.

Suggestions for Selection and Preparation of Case Material
for Group Discussion in Mental Health Conferences:
1. Why is the case selected for discussion?
2. What would be desirable goals to work toward in the discussion, such as further understanding of the patient and his or her problem, and further understanding of self (nurse) in relation to the problem?

Material That Would Be Helpful to Share with the Group:
1. Family picture—composition, ages, and so on
2. Employment and housing
3. How and when patient was referred to health department
4. Nature and extent of contacts, including number of nurses working with the patient
5. Other agencies working with the patient and the nature of their contacts (if known)
6. Major problems in terms of human relations in work with patient, family, and other agencies

Presentation of case material was followed by informal discussion. The role of the consultant was to help the group (1) decide upon priority of the patient's problems, as seen by the patient, the nurse, and the group; (2) determine to which problems the nurse could contribute particular skills and assistance; (3) assess whether help is needed from other community resources; and (4) help with methods of referral and preparation of patients for such.

Throughout the consultation conferences total participation was encouraged but the nonverbal participant was not made conspicuous. Considerable attention was given not only to the attitudes and methods of the nurse whose case was under discussion, but also to the feelings of the group in relation to the patient. Role playing was sometimes used to reenact or project an interview between nurse and patient.

In most cases, attention was given to some possible next steps the nurse might take with changed attitudes or methods resulting from group discussion. Examples might be further work with the supervisor, nursing director, or personnel in other agencies, or follow-up conferences in the mental health discussion group.

All conferences were recorded by a variety of methods, most often by a secretary taking shorthand. Summaries were made available to the total nursing staff and the consultant. The consultant also kept a record of his impressions of certain sessions. (See Appendix A for examples and recordings of consultation sessions.)

ROLE OF THE CONSULTANT

The consultant served the group through multiple roles. He brought in understanding from his own background in social work and mental health, acted as moderator, and also served as a resource person. Because of some early struggles in working together effectively, it was decided to clarify, in writing, the consultant's role in the group.

It was seen as follows:

1. To help the group increase its understanding of patients' social and emotional problems
2. To help the presenting nurses, as well as the group, to understand their own role, attitude, and techniques in working with patients and families
3. To help the group apply learning from a particular case to their general case load
4. To help use contributions from the group in working out approaches to the problem either through refinement of techniques or through new approaches
5. To help emphasize the importance of interagency cooperation and to examine ways of using other community services more effectively
6. To observe and comment on group process, when so indicated, so the group can work more effectively

In connection with the last point, a fourth workshop was held two and a half years after the monthly group consultation meetings were initiated. This workshop, which focused on group methods, grew out of the staff nurses' wish for more effective group discussion and use of the consultant. During the early sessions the consultant had encouraged the nurses to examine some of the factors affecting the effectiveness of these sessions, but prior to the workshop there had not been any focused examination of group process as such. When group sessions had not been satisfying or helpful, the nurses tended to put the responsibility on the consultant, with some direct and indirect hostility expressed for the consultant's failure to tell them what to do or how to do it.

The fourth workshop, planned by the staff with help from the consultant, was geared at an examination of interviewing as well as group process. The specific objectives in relation to group process were stated as follows: (1) to develop awareness of total group functioning; (2) to develop awareness of the individual functioning in the group; (3) to help the group assume responsibility for its own direction as to how problems were to be discussed, for continued evaluation of group performance, and for leadership; (4) to help make this a practical experience to enhance all professional group activities.

The consultant, plus staff from the state health department, served as leaders and resource people on request. As the workshop progressed, leadership shifted increasingly to the members themselves. Resultant changes in the group consultation sessions were identified as follows:

1. The group members met before the sessions to decide on the content and designate a leader, observer, and recorder from the staff.
2. The group evolved its own working definition of the consultant's role as "participating consultant." This was not a static definition, since there was periodic discussion on how the consultant might function more effectively.
3. With greater clarification of the consultant's role, there was less need for the consultant to be concerned with discussion leadership, group work methods, and structure.
4. The group assumed considerably more responsibility for the pattern, direction, and content of the discussions.
5. More consideration and planning were given to the orientation of new staff members to the sessions.
6. As the group assumed leadership roles, the sessions was increased from two to two and a half hours.
7. There was less dependence on the consultant for content and direction, in both individual and group meetings.

CONFERENCES WITH NURSING SUPERVISORS

Work with the supervisory group was similar to that with the staff groups. However, since the supervisory group was smaller, there was more opportunity for depth and easier interchange in discussions. Just as the consultant encouraged the staff nurses to use the ongoing supervisory process, so he encouraged the supervisory group to make use of the nursing director in the day-to-day operations. In addition, it was repeatedly pointed out that mental health consultation does not conflict with supervision or administration.

The content of the supervisor sessions focused mainly on supervisor–staff nurse relationships. Other topics discussed included (1) mental health implications of child health conference activity, (2) use of authority in supervisory and administrative relationships, (3) follow-up discussion of mental health conferences with staff nurses, and their appraisal, and (4) intrastaff relationships. Other problems discussed were tardiness, evaluation, excessive use of leave, personal or family problems interfering with staff performance, intrastaff friction, resistance to record-keeping, and difficulties in interagency relationships.

CONFERENCES WITH NURSING DIRECTOR

The nursing director was actively interested in consultation services for herself and her staff throughout the consultation period. In collaboration with her staff, she initiated the service, and she continued to be personally involved with it. Its success was related directly to the degree of her interest. The consultant developed a stimulating and satisfying working relationship with the director, characterized by mutual respect, confidence, and a high degree of frankness in communication.

The content of the discussion was centered on the following areas:

1. Mental health conferences with staff and supervisory nurses—planning, implementation, critical review, and efforts to integrate concepts into daily practice
2. Director–supervisor–staff nurse relationships; mental health or human relationship implications of nursing administration, including efforts to improve the emotional climate in the work setting
3. Attention to particular personal or staff problems that interfered with working relationships
4. Director's concern about her own attitudes and behavior that hindered or furthered creative use of self and staff
5. Work with related community agencies, particularly social welfare and mental health services

VARIOUS PROBLEMS

Various problems can be identified during the consultation process, both in the particular pattern of consultation and in the process in general.

One problem was the lack of continuity in staff in the group meetings. Fewer than half had participated in the three preliminary workshops, which were an important prerequisite for the consultation sessions. There were difficulties when new staff members were introduced to the group, although these were somewhat modified through orientation of new staff in regard to consultation objectives and procedures.

The interval of time between sessions required more "tuning in" on the part of consultant and group. Much might occur in the interim, both personally and professionally, both in procedures and in administrative structures, so it took some time for the consultant and group to get back into focus. Meeting more frequently would have increased the value of group consultation.

Another problem relates to voluntary versus mandatory use of the consultation. In this case there was administrative, supervisory, and professional pressure to participate. While a majority of staff found it useful and satisfying, some remained resistant to the process. It was hoped that continued exposure would decrease their reluctance. On the other hand, lack of motivation seems to be related to certain rigidities of personality and work patterns. The more fixed the patterns and attitudes, the less interest there seemed to be in the "mental health" approach.

Limited understanding of psychodynamics of behavior on the part of the staff created other difficulties. Mental health concepts can more easily be integrated into nursing practice if there is at least a minimum foundation of such knowledge prior to consultation. Yet if mental health consultation is to be important to public health nursing and other professions, a realistic effort must be initiated at whatever level of understanding is present, with the recognition that there will always be a wide range of difference in understanding in any one staff.

Other limitations in the basic public health nursing training and experience were also in evidence, since some of the problems that arose in the group discussions were not basically problems of mental health. They were often related to inadequate preparation for public health nursing as well as to limited understanding of the functions of the public health department and the nurse's role within it.

It was also noted that it is sometimes difficult for a hospital nurse to make a transition to public health nursing. In hospital nursing the emphasis is on direct nursing care and activity with patients in a protected hospital environment. Public health nurses, however, need to work with people who are free to operate with relative independence. Consequently, they must be sensitive to the meaning, in human relations terms, of doing things *for* and *to* people.

Only a limited number of individual conferences with staff nurses and supervisors could be scheduled. The consultant was to spend a day and a half per month at the local health department, in two group sessions with staff nurses, a group conference with supervisors, an individual conference with the director of nursing, and occasional individual conferences with staff or supervisors and related activities with other community agencies.

The consultant's availability for individual conferences was made explicit, and some problems might have been more appropriate for individual discussion, but it was not extensively used. About half the total staff took advantage of this opportunity. However, since time was limited, it was most effectively spent in group conferences. Similarly, with additional time and motivation, it would have been useful to follow through with the supervisors on ways of helping the staff nurse to carry out ideas discussed in the group.

Since mental health consultation depends primarily upon a relationship process, it is difficult to define meaningfully the role of the consultant before there is interaction with the consultee. Role definition must be viewed as a continuous process. There was definition prior to the consultation service, in later conferences through a written guide, and through periodic review and explanation. Nevertheless, some consultees continued to ask: "Who is he?" "Why doesn't he give us answers?" "Why doesn't the consultant tell us if we are right or wrong?" "Why doesn't he or she tell us how to do it?"

A tendency in the early phases of consultation with this care-giving group and other ones is to select the most difficult cases for discussion. Public health nurses are daily confronted with acute and chronic examples of physical, economic, social, emotional, and behavior problems. The nurses therefore tend to present cases with bizarre or extreme elements. This is understandable since such problems are troubling and time-consuming and do not lend themselves to easy solutions. In some instances these involve minority, culturally different, or impoverished groups; they are more easily discussed because we can distance ourselves from them and thereby avoid an examination of our own attitudes and behavior. In addition, emphasis on the extreme or bizarre can serve as a way of testing the consultant's "expertness," or of trying to put more responsibility on the consultant for solutions. Nevertheless, concentration on these kinds of problems does not lend itself to the most effective use of consultation. Therefore, after some initial testing and explanation, this group, and several other ones I worked with, were encouraged to present the less extreme types of problems which do make up the bulk of their work.

APPRAISAL

Consultation services should be periodically evaluated, both formally and informally. This specific service was evaluated formally after three years of monthly sessions, with the assistance of a Public Health Service mental health nurse from another region, in order to determine what changes had been brought about. The appraisal included a focused interview with each staff member who had participated. The detailed appraisal can be found in Appendix B. A brief summary of the findings is presented here.

Attitudes toward Human Behavior. There was greater understanding that behavior is caused and purposeful and therefore fulfills a need. There were fewer stereotyped generalizations about behavior in relation to cultural, racial, ethnic, and economic factors. There was also increased sensitization to emotional as well as logical motivation for behavior. Behavior was seen as sometimes being a reaction to whether or how emotional needs are being met. These positive changes related not only to patients and their families, but also to the nurse's own concept and use of self, both with other staff members and in the wider network of relationships.

Work Methods. There was increased recognition of the importance of the concept of "relationship" in work with patients. The capacity for visualizing the problem as the patient sees it deepened. There was better understanding of use of the interview as an important tool. Limitations were better accepted as an inexorable part of the working method—limitations of the patient, nurse, health department, and total community resources.

Interagency Activities. There was a good deal of increased recognition that the nurses must pool and coordinate their understanding and efforts with those of other health, welfare, education, and recreation personnel. It was also recognized that the "team" personnel had to define their goals in relation to the patient and family, and that interagency coordination had to be a dynamic effort.

Group Process. There was increased sensitization to factors of group performance which influence the effectiveness of work in groups. The group accepted more responsibility for planning, executing, and evaluating consultation sessions. Some of the methods utilized in the group mental health sessions were carried over to other group activities. Some ingredients of the group process, such as acceptance, expression of feelings, and understanding motivation, were applied to nurse–patient relationships generally, and to interviewing methods in particular.

Other Changes. Changes were also noted in improved administrator–supervisor–staff nurse relationships. In addition, some of the staff experienced personal gains as a by-product of group sessions that were not therapeutically intended. Also, motivation increased for additional training on the part of some nurses, in public health nursing generally and in mental health particularly.

Following the formal appraisal, the consultant had five conferences with the staff. The evaluation findings and implications (including summaries and impressions recorded by the nursing director and the consultant) were discussed. The staff at all levels indicated a strong desire to continue consultation. Further efforts were to be directed toward discussion of how ongoing consultation might be obtained and from what resources.*

---

*Nursing administrative staff and the health department director requested help from the consultant regarding extending mental health services in the department and community by having a full-time or part-time consultant on their staff. A full-time social worker (Coordinator of Mental Health Services) was subsequently retained, with responsibilities to include serving as consultant to the nursing staff on community-care services for the mentally ill and their families. This project was initiated on a demonstration basis with assistance from the state health department.

VIEWS OF THE PROJECT BY THE DIRECTORS OF THE SPONSORING AND CONSUMER ORGANIZATIONS

The late Charles F. Mitchell, former director of the sponsoring agency, the Division of Mental Health, Texas Department of Health, and my employer there, wrote about the importance of the project and its evaluation as follows:

> For more than a decade the Division of Mental Health carried on in-service training programs in mental health for nursing staffs of local health departments, classroom teachers, and various combinations of health, education, and welfare staffs. The objective was to strengthen and extend their understanding of mental health concepts and their application in work with people they serve, believing that this is an important activity in preventive mental health work.
>
> Considerable time was devoted to work with public health nurses because of their strategic position, both in terms of the large numbers of people they serve, especially children, and their opportunity to assist people during critical life experiences.
>
> It was found if any permanent gains were to be achieved in such training, there had to be full administrative support by the directors of the local agencies, and especially strong understanding and conscientious follow-up work by the supervisors of the staff on a long-range basis. It was also important to have maximum participation of participants both in planning and conducting the training programs.
>
> As a further development in level 2 prevention, and based on the experience in these programs, the Division set up a plan of long-time consultation and in-service education in mental health for public health nurses in three local health departments on a demonstration basis. These extended over a period of from one to three years with the hope that there would be tangible gains in:
>
> 1. The nursing staff's working knowledge of normal and pathological behavior
> 2. Use of self in helping patients deal with emotional factors in family life which affected their use of public health services, as well as early recognition of emotional disorders, with skillful referrals to appropriate agencies
> 3. Confidence, competence, and comfort in interagency efforts on behalf of families needing multiple services

Of the several consultation and in-service training projects attempted, this one seemed to work best. Therefore, the Division staff was particularly eager to have an evaluation of this project. It is thought that the evaluation will help shape our future efforts in level 2 preventive activities. While it is recognized that a "before and after," or a control group study, would have been desirable, it is thought that the present ex post facto assessment will be of immeasurable benefit in future program planning.

The staff is gratified with the outcome of the project as shown in the appraisal (Appendix B). The next step will be through consultation to the Health Department in helping work out local sources of similar consultation. This project is seen as one important step in the development of comprehensive and effective community efforts in the prevention of mental illness and the fostering of mental health.

The Director of the consumer organization was supportive of the effort throughout and welcomed the evaluation approach. He too was gratified about the outcome, particularly in light of his earlier concern about the amount of time staff invested in the consultation conferences, as is revealed in the following statement:

> I believe that the mental health consultation services have been a valuable learning experience which resulted in an improved overall nursing program and which would be worthwhile to replicate in other health departments. However, I feel that the same effective program could be carried on without using quite as many staff hours. It caused me considerable concern during its first stages because of the staff time spent and the costs of this time. I was not convinced that the benefits were commensurate with the costs. It caused me much less concern when the benefits of the services become more apparent.
>
> It appears that our nursing staff has become a more efficient group and that they have learned to work, individually and collectively, with more harmony. During the first year of the program there was some griping and displeasure, but these expressions of dissatisfaction either have disappeared or are not reaching me. It should be noted that the individuals who expressed resentment or dissatisfaction were generally those who, in my opinion, needed mental health training the most.

NECESSARY CONDITIONS FOR CONSULTATION

On the basis of this and other consultation experiences, one can generalize that there are certain requisite conditions that make the consultation process possible and facilitate its implementation. First, as was discussed in Chapter 4, there must be interest on the part of staff and administration. Furthermore, the staff must be competent within its own discipline, particularly at the supervisory and administrative levels. The staff must also be willing to use a substantial amount of material from their own case loads and working experiences.

There should be preliminary workshops in which the consultant and staff can get acquainted. These will facilitate development of a sound working relationship, provide a group experience in problem solving, and offer an opportunity to test out content and methods.

Where the background in dynamics of human behavior is particularly lacking, a certain amount of theoretical material should be presented in the workshops, or interspersed during the consultation service. Similarly, a certain amount of content about group process should also be provided by the consultant or other resource person.

Consultation sessions should be held no less than once monthly, and more frequent sessions are highly desirable. Consultation should be conducted concurrently with the staff director, supervisors, and staff. The initial effort particularly should focus on the director and supervisors.

Consultation may be carried out effectively by any of the mental health disciplines. The particular discipline and the staff's relationship to it, however, make for significant differences in the nature of the service provided. The consultant needs a working knowledge and respect for the profession with which she or he is working, both theoretically and through direct observation of professional practice.

As has been emphasized, the effectiveness of consultation is dependent primarily on a relationship process, and therefore the relationship between consultant and consultee group must be based on acceptance, mutual respect, and freedom to reveal professional feelings and functioning.

Evaluation should be built in as part of the consultation service at the time of its inception. Although assessment of change as a result of consultation is difficult, nevertheless some attempt should be made to measure change in the consultee group in relation to attitudes toward clients, interviewing skills, performance in group, program/administration and intrastaff and interagency relationships, and other such matters.

CHAPTER 6

A Study of Consultation Services in Eight Community Mental Health Centers

INTRODUCTION

Specific purposes of the study will be given in the next section, but in general the study was done to learn what effects budget cuts in the early 1980s had on consultation and to get a sampling of staff attitudes about the importance of consultation and educational preparation for it.

Sources of information were interviews with nineteen professional staff and one board member at six centers in Texas and one center each in Wyoming and Ohio. The centers were a good mix of urban and rural locations and varied staff sizes. In a majority of the centers studied, consultation services were sacrificed, in some drastically, for direct care, especially for the severely mentally ill. In others consultation not only was maintained at previous levels but increased.

A composite picture is presented of consultation views and activities rather than individual descriptions and identification of these centers. This is for reasons of confidentiality and protection, since some funding sources no longer regarded consultation as a high priority or an item eligible for reimbursement.

Although views about the importance and nature of consultation varied considerably among the twenty persons interviewed, none regarded consultation

A brief version of the study was presented at the annual meeting of the American Public Health Association, Mental Health Section, Anaheim, California, November 12, 1984.

The author is grateful for financial support of the Texas portion of the study provided by the Hogg Foundation for Mental Health, Wayne H. Holtzman, President, The University of Texas, Austin; and for research incentive funds from The College of Public and Community Services, George F. Nickolaus, Dean, The University of Missouri–Columbia.

as unneeded or unimportant. Still, a few seemed uneasy talking about it as something they do, formally or informally. The reason, perhaps, was concern that funding from some sources might be threatened. Although I will not name the centers or respondents, for these reasons, I am most grateful for their contributions.

Only a limited amount of time could be given to center visits. Interviews at the centers ranged from one to five hours, with the average about two and a half hours. This obviously was very little time to cover a complex topic for the stated purposes.

Added to the time problem was the fact that often before we got to questions about the current "state of the art," an amount of time had to be spent clarifying definitions of consultation. What some presented as "consultation" represented for me another kind of service activity—collaboration or coordination.

An additional restraint was that I could talk with only a small number of people at each center and so may not have gotten a representative picture of attitudes and operations at some centers. At three of the centers, contact was limited to one person; at the other five centers, the number of participants was two, three, three, four, and five.

PURPOSES OF THE STUDY

While working first with the Division of Mental Health, Texas State Department of Health, and later for the Department of Mental Health and Mental Retardation in the 1960s, I assisted as a consultant in the organization of three of the six centers described in the Texas portion of this study. I planned to visit two others that I helped to organize, but one of them reported that it is currently providing no consultation services. The other one misunderstood my request, thinking that I was seeking information about how they use consultation instead of how (and to whom) they provide it.

The three centers visited that I helped to organize were initiated and funded on the basis that they would devote substantial time to consultation activities. In fact, one of them, as part of the understanding with the state departments (first Health then MHMR) for funding purposes, agreed to devote 50 percent of staff time to consultation, education, community organization, and related indirect services.

There were several purposes for this study:

1. To survey current attitudes about the importance of mental health consultation and the nature and volume of consultation services offered at eight community centers.
2. To learn what effects recent budget cuts and constraints have had on consultation services in Texas and two other states.

3. To attempt to test, through these visits, whether many of my earlier assumptions about consultation were valid.

4. To gather information from respondents about what they think is required in basic and continuing education for provision of consultation services, what preparation they had, what they would have liked, suggestions as to how consultation might best be taught, and references that have been helpful to them.

5. To add to my own body of knowledge about consultation through discussions with other seasoned mental health consultants.

STUDY QUESTIONS

The following items were presented verbally. There was some variation in the items presented due to the amount of time that could be spent at each center and the nature of responses in the early parts of the interviews.

1. Brief description of the center: populations served, budget, staff, sources of support, and so on.

2. How is consultation valued, especially in relation to direct services?

3. How much time is spent in consultation in comparison with direct services?

4. Brief description of the consultation program, including audiences, how selected, how entry is made, methods, evaluations, and related information (the "why," "what," "how" and "the doing").

5. What have been some of the major problems in provision of consultation services?

6. Has consultation been "marketed," and if so, how and with what results?

7. Commentary on preparation for consultation, both in basic professional education and continuing education. Included with this item were questions about respondents' preparation, what they would have liked, what they got, and particular references or individuals that influenced their learning about consultation. A related question was addressed to what they saw as preferred methods, in both basic and continuing education for consultation.

It was necessary to vary interview content and method at three of the centers, where current consultation activity was quite minimal and in one case almost nonexistent. Here it seemed reasonable to focus on educational activities, since these are closely related to consultation and regarded by some (Gallessich, 1982) as one form of consultation. In the centers where consultation is extremely minimal I thought it important to spend the time discussing both consultation and education.

The 20 respondents were as follows:

Center	*Titles*
1. _____	Director of Outpatient Services
2. _____	Director
	Coordinators of C&E (2)
	Supervisor of C&E
	Management and Planning Coordinator
3. _____	Director
	Manager of Special Services
	Community Education Specialist
	Manager of Consumer Credit Counseling
4. _____	Director
5. _____	Director
	Assistant Director
	Board Member
6. _____	Program Director
7. _____	Executive Director
	Director of Prevention and Marketing
	Clinical Director
8. _____	Associate Director
	Coordinator of C&E Service

PROFILES OF CENTERS

As is outlined in Table 6.1, there is a great range in populations served (130,000 to 1.5 million); budgets ($0.75 million to $14.34 million); and numbers of staff (32 to 474). Three of the centers serve large metropolitan areas; two are in medium sized cities; three are in small cities and provide services for from three to six counties.

CONSULTATION ACTIVITIES

Purposes

Generally, consultation as carried out in these centers is for the purpose of assisting workers in other human service organizations with client diagnosis, interventive methods, case finding, treatment, and collaboration. It is an indirect service for preventive purposes at primary, secondary, and tertiary levels.

TABLE 6.1. PROFILE OF CENTERS

Center	Populations Served	Budgets[a] (in millions)	Staff
1	1,500,000	$14.34	474
2	420,000	6.5	280
3	350,000	2.5	21[b]
4	250,000	3	132
5	240,000	4	180
6	150,000	.75	32
7	(not available)	3.25	120
8	130,000	2	70

[a] Figures are approximate and projected for 1983.
[b] The small number of staff is accounted for by this center's purchase of most client services from other agencies. The 21 staff provide administrative, consultation and education, finance, development, management, support, and related services.

Representative of purposes is the following mission statement from one of the centers, covering both consultation and education services:

> To promote human development through prevention with the general population and populations at risk; improving the effectiveness of mental health and human services; facilitating establishment of linkages within and between the programs; and increasing the awareness of the community about psychological and developmental problems and the approaches to prevention and treatment of such problems.

Additional purposes include assistance with design and improvement of agency programs, administration, and community development of services.

Separate or Adjunct Service

In five of the centers, consultation is a separate, identifiable service within the administrative structure. In three it is an adjunct service. In one of these, however, before the current serious financial constraints, it had been a separate service with this statement justifying the separateness:

> Within the CMHC network, consultation and education should be a visible, identifiable service within that administrative structure and one that is accountable to the overall administration of the center.

I support this statement, and it is my distinct impression from observation of consultation activities in Texas and other states that where consultation is a separate unit it is carried out most successfully and in the largest volume.

Audiences

Although the following is not an exhaustive list, it is a representative one of persons served through consultation in these agencies and organizations:

Human resources (welfare)	Sheltered workshops
Schools	Aging
Colleges and universities	Probation and parole
Head Start	Corrections
Health	Courts
Nursing homes	Day care
Police	Business and industry
Churches	

It was my impression that welfare agencies are the largest recipients of consultation services from the eight centers. Consultation on protection, abuse, and adoption problems and procedures are the most prevalent within this category.

Attitudes

There is considerable variation in attitude among the eight centers about the importance of consultation, competence of staff to provide it, marketing the product, and collection of fees for consultation and educational services. Most of the centers do not charge for C&E services. In one center they do not think they could compete with private practitioners if they were to charge. In several others there is some concern about charging because of sensitivity to criticism for receiving both tax support and fees. Such conflict, however, does not exist in relation to fees for direct services to clients.

Three of the centers market C&E services quite aggressively and collect significant income from them. At one center, in Texas, income for C&E services increased in less than three years from $14,000 to $40,000 per year. The center studied in Ohio did systematic studies of C&E needs and then actively marketed programs, which resulted in an increase of C&E revenues by 400 percent in one year, from $2,000 to $40,000. Their goal was to increase such income to $60,000 annually. The dramatic increase in revenue occurred in spite of the fact that the equivalency of twelve C&E persons, before budget losses, was reduced to five.

It was difficult to get accurate amounts of time devoted to consultation because at most centers no counting of time is made, since it is not a reimbursable item from the state. At one center, lumping C&E together, it is estimated that 5 to 10 percent of total staff time is devoted to the combined services. At another center, which collects significant income for both C&E services, careful separate statistics are kept on both kinds of services. Table 6.2

TABLE 6.2. CONSULTATION CONTACTS BY KIND

Type	Total	% Total
Client Centered	1,914	78
Community Education Training	170	7
Consumer Education	122	5
Agency Centered	97	4
Community Centered	37	4
Consultee Centered	41	2

illustrates, for the year prior to the study, the number of its consultation contacts according to type of consultation.

At one center in Texas, which devoted considerable time to educational services but little to consultation, some staff believe that most of the personnel are not competent to provide consultation for other human service providers; many are paraprofessionals. Most practitioners in medicine, law, and the clergy, for example, do not seek out the center for consultation services but go to the private sector for them. In addition, I was told that staff at this center lack skills in making entree into other human service organizations. It was also reported that staff are not innovative and are basically conservative, particularly about nondirect services.

Problems

One center in Texas, which had had a large C&E unit before drastic budget cuts and a 50% reduction in staff, no longer has C&E as a separate unit but keeps it only as an adjunctive service. This center, in a large urban area, devotes 95 percent of its time to the seriously mentally ill, including 4,700 dischargees from a state hospital the previous year. Case loads vary between 100 to 400 per staff member. Services to children were cut by 40 percent. Consultation services are now almost nonexistent, and what educational services are provided are mostly interpretive in nature, that is, they describe the center's program and services. Education of a preventive kind for the general public and populations at risk, except for the seriously mentally ill, is extremely limited. The center once had a far-reaching educational program for the general public and for numerous service providers, both public and private.

A second Texas center had to reduce staff numbers by 20 percent. Others seemed to be holding their own, but C&E services had been drastically reduced in four of them, and case loads of the seriously mentally ill increased. There is great variation, however, in percentage of the seriously mentally ill served. In one smaller center this was estimated to be about 15 percent, while in another large center it is 95 percent. The larger proportion of case loads of the seriously mentally ill occurs more in the larger urban areas.

Direct services, especially to the seriously mentally ill, were high-priority items within the Texas state system, and centers were rewarded financially for such services. State reimbursement was not provided for C&E services. Support for C&E must come from fees and other local sources, except in those few centers where federal funds were still available (1983) for them. These were rapidly declining and expected to expire soon.

Although C&E services were regarded as important in varying degrees at all Texas centers in the study, consultation in particular had been drastically reduced except at two centers in rural areas. One got the feeling also that where consultation had been continued, even in very modest amounts, it was done on a sort of "bootleg" or "underground" basis. At one of the larger centers, staff believed that significant amounts of consultation were still provided but on a "very informal" basis. They were not counted because they were not reimbursable items. As one director said: "You put your time where your money comes from. Consultation is not in the state computer."

One of the other larger Texas centers formerly had two distinct C&E units, with five staff members assigned to each. At the time of the study it had only one unit with two staff assigned to it.

A GLIMPSE AT CONSULTATION SERVICES IN A MULTI-COUNTY WYOMING MENTAL HEALTH CENTER

Rationale for the Visit

The visit was made in order to enlarge the sampling of consultation activities in mental health centers. Wyoming, like Texas, is an energy-rich state which had experienced rapid population growth during the past decade. Unfortunately, because of schedule constraints, the visit to this center was a very brief one and was limited to contact with only one of four offices serving a multi-county area.

I also made the visit because of a special interest in centers that serve small cities and broad, sparsely populated rural areas. Wyoming was of interest too because of work that had been done there in development of mental health and other human services for residents of boom towns during the late 1970s and early 1980s. Boom towns brought mixed blessings—more money, more jobs, more taxes, and new ideas, but with these came staggering increases in child abuse, family disturbance, substance abuse, and crimes against persons. Although there were rapid and substantial population increases, case loads of mental health and other human services centers grew far out of proportion to the population.

In their book (1980) the Davenports underlined the unhappy fact that the ability to extract and process mineral riches was not matched by the ability to deal with the social consequences and human costs of rapid growth and development. Weisz, in the same book (p. 55), cited the 1974–78 boom in Gillette, Wyoming, marked by a 610 percent increase in admissions to the state hospital while the county population increased only 62 percent.

Fortunately, some foresighted professors from the University of Wyoming, with the help of a training grant from the National Institute of Mental Health, were able to intervene with boom town problems through the Wyoming Human Services Project. They developed innovative training procedures for students in social work and related human services for both planning and direct services in energy-impacted communities. The training, consultation, and educational efforts also resulted in the production of a reservoir of personnel to provide ongoing services to communities.

These efforts are exemplary and represent legitimate "quality of life" concerns for mental health personnel. As I have said elsewhere (Rieman, 1982), the project as well as books (Davenport & Davenport, 1980) and other writings about it are significant contributions to knowledge in pioneering areas of stress prevention and control.

A serendipitous benefit from the visit to this Wyoming mental health center was the discovery of the center's historical strong interest in preventive activities. An activity of special interest and timeliness was one directed at suicide prevention among teenagers, which will be described later in the chapter.

Another serendipitous benefit was the discovery of two important unpublished documents about mental health policy making and changes at the state level. Eighteen states, including Wyoming, were studied in relation to priority issues defined by policy makers at the top levels. The documents compared states in regard to about fifteen issues ranging from services to the chronically ill to provision of preventive services (Rich, August and November 1982). A later section of this chapter gives information about policy makers' attitudes in Wyoming and comparisons with other states, with special attention to preventive services.

Center Profile

Information about the center and its consultation activities was obtained in an interview of about one and a half hours with the Associate Director (psychologist) and the Coordinator of Consultation and Education Services (social worker). At the time of the study the Associate Director had been with the center for ten years and the Coordinator, twelve years. The Coordinator devoted about 20 percent of his time to C&E activities.

The center, organized in 1962, has offices in four small cities and serves a population of 130,000 in four counties. The budget of approximately $2.25 million comes from city, county, United Way, and state sources and fees for services. State payments are made on a population formula basis. State payments increased from $30,000 yearly in 1970 to $1,333,461 for fiscal year 1983–84. This increase permitted placement of staff in all four counties, substantially increased case loads and services, and reduced local and state hospital admissions. The four-county center staff now consists of fifty professionals and twenty support personnel.

Center services that are state supported include outpatient, liaison with state hospital, and partial care for the chronically mentally ill. The state also supports substance abuse programs for detoxification, direct service, residential service, and prevention.

Interestingly, when the center was first organized, and for about two years thereafter, services were exclusively prevention, through consultation and education with various care-givers and organizations. There is a historical center mission statement which gave the rationale for this, and which my informants remembered seeing but were unable to locate. It is assumed however, that with a very limited budget, concentration on preventive services seemed to be the most logical expenditure of funds. There was a similar early policy of the Division of Mental Health in Texas.

Consultation Activities

In the central office and the three additional county offices, consultation and education are carried out as adjunct services. Although no exact statistics were available regarding the amount of time staff devoted overall to consultation and education, a reasonable estimate was 10 percent. This estimate does not include substance abuse preventive services, which represent a significant amount of time.

The quantity and quality of consultation services vary considerably among the four offices. Some have better access to consultees, such as school staffs. Consultation is provided for all human service agencies in all counties. In the largest city, consultation (group) is also provided for public health nurses. Some services are provided for clergymen.

Children's protective services, as in Texas, are heavy consumers of consultation through both formal and informal methods. The schools are also substantial consumers. With some there are formal contracts, and charges are made on an hourly basis. There is also an arrangement with Head Start personnel for weekly case and program consultation, reimbursed by the hour, with directors, nurses, and other staff. There is considerable "informal consultation" provided for both individuals and groups which is not paid for.

A free consultation service was provided by the center for University of Wyoming administrators the year prior to the study for development of student emergency mental health services.

In only one office had consultation services been recently reduced, in the largest city of the four. A similar pattern was observed in Texas, where centers serving smaller cities and more rural populations provided the largest amounts of consultation and education activities.

In the Wyoming center, consultation services are better accepted in rural areas. There seems to be less stigma attached to them, as compared with direct services. In sparsely populated areas other human services are extremely limited and mental health may even be the "only game in town."

Consultation and education were rewarded financially from state sources in the area of substance abuse programs. One of these is in a facility that focuses on prevention and early intervention. Services of two staff members, and half time of a third, are devoted exclusively to consultation and education activities. The facility, open to all youth and their parents, provides opportunities for them to discover positive, nonchemical alternatives to substance abuse. Consultation on an ongoing basis is also given to many community organizations, clubs, and social groups. The media are provided with information and educational materials on substance abuse control and prevention strategies.

Center offices in the four counties had considerable flexibility and encouragement to do consultation, but sometimes indirect services have to be cut back at some offices if "direct services are suffering."

Informants expressed concern about conflicts between formal and informal consultation, with a strong stated preference for formal, well-spelled-out agreements. However, too many of the consultation arrangements were still "informal." Concern was also expressed about the serious limitations of one-time consultations.

A very interesting and exemplary consultation and education project was one on suicide prevention. During the spring of 1982 there was an "epidemic" of four adolescent suicides in three weeks in one city served by the center. Along with the shock and sadness experienced by community residents, there were serious concerns about contagiousness of suicide and the fear that a larger epidemic might develop. The mental health center responded by organizing and implementing, without charge, suicide prevention and crisis control workshops and consultations for school administrators, psychologists, social workers, nurses, counselors, and others. The center also responded to over a dozen requests from organizations, and the media, for specialized information and training on suicide prevention.

There were no further suicides during the remaining school year. However, the center did receive about a call a day regarding youngsters who made suicide threats, gestures, or attempts.

By coincidence, as this report on the Wyoming mental health center was being written, the following newspaper story appeared about a similar "epidemic" in Plano, Texas (*Columbia Missourian*, August 26, 1983). Community response, as in the Wyoming city, is described including the involvement of mental health personnel:

Teen Suicides Prompt Community Action

Plano, Texas (UPI)–Three teenage suicides in a week and six since February have convulsed an affluent community north of Dallas.

"Now we have to live this down," said Wendy Compton, 16, a junior at Plano High School, on Thursday. "The last two were friends of mine and it upsets me that these people, good people, killed themselves."

Scott Difiglia, 18, died Tuesday, a day after he put a bullet in his brain in depression over breaking up with his girlfriend.

John Gundlah, 17, died a week earlier with his girlfriend, Mary Jacobs, 17. They sat in a car with the motor running in a closed garage because they were told to ease off on their close relationship.

Three young men killed themselves in February and March, the first out of grief over a drag-racing accident in which another student died, and the other two reportedly because they felt pressured about their futures.

"There's so much affluence, so much pressure," said James Prudhome, 17, a senior.

Parents have deluged a suicide hotline in recent weeks and are organizing a crisis center which will be made up of mental health professionals and volunteers to help troubled children and parents.

Plano is a business boom town of 90,000, with 50,000 of the residents arriving during the past fifteen years.

"We have family problems and a high divorce rate," said Larry Quinn, director of activities at the sprawling high school, enrollment 2,300.

"But a lot of other communities are experiencing the same things. We're not worse. In many ways we feel we're better. That's what's so frustrating and puzzling."

He said Plano's two high schools have an active network of parent and student support groups, including a program called "Students Working All Together."

"This program began before the suicides, but it began because of concern over the large campus atmosphere," said Plano school district spokeswoman Trish Torgersen. "Now we know we need these programs more than ever."

These events in two cities many hundreds of miles apart make one wonder what significance there may be, nationally, about "contagion" and volume of suicide among teenagers. They also point up the importance of exchanging knowledge and of networking among centers in the design and operation of both preventive and treatment programs.

PREVENTION—THE MELODY LINGERS ON

When the Wyoming center began operations in 1962, it offered preventive services exclusively. Although preventive services now occupy only about 10 percent of total staff time, they are regarded as important community services.

They are provided in significant volume, in a wide range of forms, and for a variety of consumers. The volume is proportionately greater in the more sparsely populated areas.

Several papers by Rich (August and November, 1982) discuss Wyoming policy makers' attitudes regarding prevention. The prevention "melody" (and song), as revealed in these papers, do linger on in Wyoming and will be illustrated through brief excerpts from the Rich studies, which concern mental health policy issues in eighteen states, including Wyoming.*

Stakeholders in mental health policy-making systems were interviewed, in the spring of 1980 and again in the spring of 1982, about policy issues and priorities. Policy makers included legislators, officials in mental health departments and other human service agencies, health planners, state and county level service providers, and others. In the spring of 1982, 336 individuals were asked to rate, from 0 (low) to 3 (high), the priority of the following issues at the state level.

- Provision of services to the chronically ill
- Fiscal accountability
- Coordination between institution and community programs
- Attracting third-party reimbursement
- Shifting state resources from institution to community
- Provision of services to the elderly mentally ill
- Changing Medicare and Medicaid formulas for reimbursement
- Increased service integration with health care systems
- Accountability of mental health officials to public on treatment issues
- Favorable zoning regulations for community facilities
- Increasing Title XX funds for mental health services
- Provision of services to veterans
- Provision of preventive services
- Disputes among mental health professionals—who should be reimbursed for mental health services

The orderings differed slightly from state to state, but the key issues remained about the same (Rich, November 1982). What emerged as "high priority" in each state were grouped into four categories:

- Delivery of services to two key target groups—the chronically mentally ill and the youth and/or elderly
- Issues related to financing the mental health system

---

*Arizona, Idaho, Indiana, Iowa, Kentucky, Massachusetts, New Jersey, New Mexico, Oregon, Rhode Island, South Carolina, South Dakota, Tennessee, Virginia, Washington, Wisconsin, Wyoming, and the District of Columbia.

- Integration of the system—unifying the various components
- Issues related to making the system and its professionals accountable, both fiscally and in treatment outcomes.

Prevention did not receive a high priority in any of the states. In fact it was third from the bottom; only provision of services to veterans and disputes among mental health professionals were ranked lower. Wyoming rated provision of preventive services 1.9 in 1980 and 2.1 in 1982. The average for all states was 1.7 both years.

In rating of provision of preventive services, Wyoming ranked fourth among the eighteen states in 1980, and in 1982 it tied another state for third. It was among the few states of the eighteen that increased its rating of preventive services between 1980 and 1982.

One of several statements used in the study to test attitudes toward preventive programs was this:

Since we do not know enough about prevention, mental health programs should direct their prime efforts toward treating the mentally ill rather than developing prevention programs.

The eighteen states were asked to react on a scale of 1 to 4, from "strongly agree" to "strongly disagree." Wyoming's score (3.9, "somewhat disagree") was sixth from the highest, the highest being 3.43 (Rich, November 1982).

Although prevention no longer has a high priority on the mental health policy agenda in any of these states, being replaced mostly by a concern for the chronically mentally ill, these statements from Rich (August 1982) seem to be quite significant and also somewhat hopeful for prevention:

The fact that prevention has a lower priority is not an invitation to declare the CMHC movement a failure or to reject the emphasis on "prevention" and preventative programs over the last twenty years . . . . Apparently, the stakeholders in the mental health system are not prepared to delimit the system by ceasing to develop prevention programs. (pp. 54, 56)

One commissioner reported:

I think shrinkage is likely to occur in the areas of outpatient services for non-severely mentally ill people, for the people who are perhaps using marriage counseling and other kinds of services. I think that's unfortunate, because I think they are highly valued services by the community and they build a lot of goodwill for us and support. They also make people aware of mental health programs and also they do a lot in the preventive sense. (p. 74)

Rich (November 1982) concludes:

These data characterize the dilemma faced by state and local mental health policy makers. They support the goals of the community mental health "movement" and, in particular, the goal of emphasizing primary prevention. Policy stakeholders are not prepared to label the prevention priority or the CMHC's as a failure. However, they are also not prepared at least at this time to attach a high priority to the area of primary or secondary prevention.

Other conclusions (Rich, November 1982) point up the gap between the priority and support for prevention philosophy and some key policy issues as follows:

- State policy makers are not sure of what constitutes "success" in the area of prevention or of how to measure it.
- How does one hold prevention programs accountable—in both fiscal and programmatic terms?
- What should be the tradeoff between prevention which is ambiguous and treatment of the chronically mentally ill who have very specific and concrete needs? What should this tradeoff be in an environment of scarce financial resources?

Before the gap can be closed, Rich says, these questions will have to be addressed.

PREPARATION FOR CONSULTATION

All respondents in Texas agreed that graduate education for mental health professionals should include consultation content. There were differences, however, about amount, method, and whether some traditional curriculum content could be sacrificed to make room for consultation theory and practice. One psychologist felt that some information on consultation should be offered at the beginning of graduate training. Beyond theory, the preferred model for teaching skills would be through first observing others do consultation and then doing it under supervision. He felt that there is a lot of "clutter" in graduate training, and if this were removed consultation could easily be accommodated. He was critical also of education in his discipline being "academic training rather than performance training." "Academic centers do not train practitioners, they train academics," he said.

A second respondent, a social worker, had some good but brief exposure to consultation during his graduate field placement but received nothing from the campus. He would have liked to have had educational content on both theory and application, especially on "what it is" and "how to do it." He said that at least one of the four semesters of graduate training was "waste," including several introductory courses. He would have preferred more electives. Consultation theory should begin, he said, in the first semester and be taught throughout, including in the field placement. To teach consultation properly, he felt, there should be at least two mandatory courses plus one or two electives. Learning in school and on the job can be done most effectively through observation, as an apprentice and through collaboration. Theory and practice should be closely related. Most of his learning occurred on the job through the procedures described above.

A third respondent, a social worker, had had some limited exposure to consultation during graduate training but said, "It took me twelve years to have an opportunity to use what I learned in school." He strongly favored consultation training during graduate training at least to the extent of some introductory or survey courses. Just as important as learning how to do consultation, he said, is "learning how to use it."

A fourth respondent, another social worker, thought consultation should be incorporated with other courses. He would not eliminate traditional content to do it, however. Instead he thought that a third year, or at least an additional semester, should be added to the two-year program to allow study of special kinds of service delivery such as consultation. Role playing to him is a preferred method for teaching consultation. Describing desirable characteristics of consultants, he cited: having less need (than the clinician) to be in control, the ability to think quickly on their feet, and the ability to synthesize. He further described the consultant as a "prospector" and "highly ethical huckster." The consultant must of course be comfortable in work with groups and with a great variety of groups, from the "Brown Berets to the Junior League." This respondent too had little exposure to consultation in school, and what he learned came on the job, in discussion with other consultants, and through networking.

The fifth respondent in Texas, also a social worker, is director of a center that provides significant amounts of consultation services and produces substantial income from them. He had special training in consultation in graduate school and beyond as observer, apprentice, and "doer" under supervision. He was the recipient of a scholarship for graduate training from the Division of Mental Health, Texas Department of Health, while I was employed there; the Division arranged special content for him, plus extensive exposure to consultation through association with staff members of the Division who were providing many kinds of this service. He considered this training opportunity a valuable experience, one that has greatly influenced his consultation and administrative styles, both in his current position (three years at the time of the study) and for twelve years as director of another center. Even though this training occurred a number of years ago, we both viewed it as a model for current teaching of consultation in school and beyond.

Respondents, perhaps because of lack of time to think about it during the brief interview, had difficulty recalling specific references that had been particularly useful to them. One respondent named as an exemplary reference book, "The Profession and Practice of Consultation" (Gallessich, 1982).

In an abstract of a doctoral dissertation, "Competency Based Guidelines for the Training and Development of Consultation and Education Specialists in Community Mental Health Centers" (Raber, 1982) is this statement: "In summary, the field of education in consultation is in its infancy in terms of clear training models."

Iscoe (1983) also refers to current confusion about the role of consultants and the "underemphasis of consultation in the curriculum in most training programs for psychologists." He says further: "Effective consultation is a skillful process requiring a combination of backgrounds and skills every bit as demanding as that going into the making of an effective therapist."

Although in the Wyoming center, educational preparation was discussed only briefly and with only two of the Wyoming center's staff, the responses are important. They are also generally consistent with responses from the Texas study. The social worker said that consultation concepts can and should be taught during graduate training. The first year, he thought, should include a survey course, with a more specialized one during the second year. He felt too that course content should be focused exclusively on consultation rather than being combined with some other subject matter such as administration or supervision. He could recall only a two- or three-day "course" during his graduate education, given by an "outside" teacher. The content was good but limited. Since then he has had a few, but meaningful, learning experiences through continuing education workshops.

The psychologist respondent recalled some brief content on consultation during his graduate training as part of a one-year course on community mental health. Most of his learning, as was true for the majority of respondents in the Texas study, occurred through observing and doing "on the job." He felt that even mental health personnel who would not be doing very much consultation should have some academic exposure to it to assist them in their planning and other clinical functions.

Teaching content, this psychologist said, should include not only basic definitions and principles but the many possible pitfalls in provision and use of consultation. He cited serving as a co-consultant or apprentice as a good way of learning consultation procedures. A good combination, he felt, would be consultation content allied with that on management. He recalled no references on consultation that were particularly useful.

SUMMARY

Although the study was for me a bittersweet experience in some ways, especially in Texas, the purposes for which it was made were largely met. First, I was able to visit eight mental health centers briefly and had an opportunity to discuss consultation and the "current state of the art" with nineteen staff members of various disciplines, and one board member.

The second purpose, to learn the effects of budget cuts and other constraints on consultation services, was fulfilled, as was the third, which was to verify or validate through these visits earlier assumptions about consultation theory and practice.

A fourth purpose was to get a sampling of views about the importance of training for consultation and how and when it might be done. I got a good sampling from several disciplines which should be of interest to educators. Chapter 9 offers a further discussion of education.

Only one of five major purposes was not met to a significant degree. I learned a great deal about what is going on, or not going on, in consultation, but I was not able to learn much that was new to me. Had there been more time to talk with respondents and to observe consultation at the several centers, undoubtedly some learning would have occurred.

Severe financial constraints and increased emphasis on services for the seriously mentally ill caused a drastic reduction in consultation services in half of the centers visited. Because of a national study I had concluded just previously, *Notable Solutions to Problems in Mental Health Services Delivery* (Rieman, Cravens, & Stroul, 1985), I expected to find such reductions because they were occurring in many parts of the country for similar reasons, but it was not a pleasant experience to have it confirmed. There are many exemplary practices in operation around the country in meeting budget, leadership, organization, service, and related problems, but consultation and education services have been seriously curtailed. This is an unfortunate and short-sighted "solution" to fiscal and related problems, and eventually we will pay dearly for reductions in these services. I said in a paper presentation (Rieman, 1988) which summarized the *Notable Solutions* study above:

> Mental illness will be for the foreseeable future a very serious and perhaps increasing problem. Massive efforts and funding from many sources are needed for prevention, remediation, education, and research. Several of the centers in the study reported that they are so busy with the "doing," and with "survival," that they don't have time to look carefully at what they are doing, why they are doing it, research it or even describe it. *Is survival enough?* (p. 19)

Perhaps eight centers is not enough of a sampling to infer any correlation between administrative attitude about the importance of consultation and the current state of this practice. Although there are other factors involved, I did have the impression that where there is deep administrative and board commitment to this service as an integral part of community mental health efforts, ways are found to protect it and even increase it through aggressive marketing and collecting of fees. Some centers are conflicted about charging fees. However, three of the centers described made significant increases in collections for such service.

Conflict about fee collection for consultation is conveyed in excerpts of what seems to be a rather apologetic statement in a Rural Community Mental Health Newsletter (Riggs, 1983).

> For years we have talked about lobbying effectively. Now the catch word is "marketing." What is the future of the CMH ideal, when we turn to EAP's, the selling of consultation . . .? (p. 3)

A later quote from the same source, however, expresses a concern that I share:

> Perhaps the era of comprehensive community mental health services is over, to be replaced by the private sector and state funded chronic care centers. (p. 3)

In the *Notable Solutions* study (Rieman et al., 1985) I identified several mental health centers that not only had managed to maintain previous levels of consultation and education services but had significantly increased them. One in Ohio increased its income from these services some 400 percent in a year, through careful market research, skillful promotion of quality products, and unhesitatingly charging reasonable fees, as is done for "hands on" services everywhere.

For the seriously or chronically mentally ill, it would seem to be a wise expenditure of funds and staff resources to use clinicians who are also skilled in consultation and education, to train and consult with paraprofessionals. This is being done on an extensive basis in several places in Wisconsin (Rieman et al., 1985). It may not be economically efficient to use highly skilled clinicians for this group. Frequently therapeutic services are not what are most needed, and in some instances they can even be damaging. However, an extensive range and volume of supportive services of many kinds are needed. These can be given by (less expensive) paraprofessionals and others if skilled supervision, consultation, and educational services are provided for them.

Elsewhere (Wagenfeld, Lemkau, & Justice, 1982), I argue not only for maintaining consultation at current levels but for increasing it:

> A further argument for extending consultation and education activities is that even if there were more specialists, many nonspecialized personnel are in more natural and strategic positions—often during times of crisis—to help those

with whom they are in frequent contact. With traditional diagnostic and treatment approaches, we but dent the total problem. Mental health professions need allies to carry out large-scale preventive, education, and treatment activities. Consultation and education can help develop and extend the skills of our allies.

Improved and extended services for the chronically and seriously mentally ill are needed in Texas and nationally on a massive basis. But Texas, where most of this study was done, can afford services for this *and other* populations "at risk" and an array of preventive and educational services for the population at large. Hise (1983) says:

> Texas ranks fourth in the nation in tax capacity, but lowest in the nation in tax effort, as compared to its capacity.

Paradoxically Texas was also one of the lower contributors in the nation to human services in per capita dollars. At the time of this study the problem there and in other states seemed to be one of public attitude, priority, and commitment, not lack of tax potential.

REFERENCES

Davenport, J. A., & Davenport, J., III (Eds.). (1980). *The boom town: Problems and promises in the energy vortex.* Laramie: University of Wyoming.

Gallessich, J. (1982). *The profession and practice of consultation.* San Francisco: Jossey-Bass.

Hise, H. W. (1983, March). A tax increase or a decrease in human services. *The Curriculor*, Texas Council of Community MHMR Centers, 1–7.

Iscoe, I. (1983). *Mental health consultation and education.* Unpublished paper, University of Texas, Austin.

Raber, R. F. (1982). *Competency based guidelines for the training and development of consultation and education specialists in community mental health centers.* Abstract, doctoral dissertation, Kansas State University, Manhattan, Kans.

Rich, R. F. (1982, November). *Implementing new mental health policy priorities at the state level.* Paper presented at the Conference on "Implementing the Prevention Priority: Goals, Policies, Programs" at Carnegie-Mellon University. (Research presented in this paper was sponsored by the National Institute of Mental Health Grant Nos. MH-30791 and MH-37799.)

Rich, R. F. (1982, August). *Interim report: Mental health policy making at the state and federal levels: Challenges for the 1980's.* Paper presented at the Ninetieth Annual Convention of the American Psychological Association, Washington, D.C. (The research presented in this paper was funded by the National Institute of Mental Health, Grant Nos. MH-30791 and MH-37799).

Rieman, D. W. (1982). Changing practices in personnel preparation and use. In M.

Wagenfeld, P. Lemkau, & B. Justice (Eds.), *Public mental health: Perspectives and prospects* (p. 175). Beverly Hills, Calif: Sage Publications.

Rieman, D. W. (1988). Study of *examplary practices in organization and delivery of community mental health services*. Paper presented at the Council on Social Work Education, Annual Program Meeting, Atlanta, Ga.

Rieman, D. W., Cravens, R., & Stroul, B. (1985). *Notable solutions to problems in mental health services delivery*. National Institute of Mental Health, Rockville, Md.

Riggs, R. (1983, Spring). *Rural mental health newsletter,* p. 3.

Wagenfeld, M., Lemkau, P., & Justice, B. (Eds.). (1982). *Public mental health: Perspectives and prospects* (pp. 1–6). Beverly Hills, Calif.: Sage Publications.

Weisz, R. (1980). In J. A. Davenport & J. Davenport, III (Eds.), *The boom town: Problems and promises in the energy vortex*. Laramie: University of Wyoming.

PART III
Issues and Recommendations

CHAPTER 7

Ethics in Consultation

The importance of consultation, because of its multiplier effects, will no doubt continue to grow in the 1990s as human support resources will likely decline and social, health, and economic problems will mount. Yet, because of the deficits in basic and continuing education for consultation (see Chapters 6 and 9), many social workers are ill prepared for consultation practice. Further, *ethics* of the practice receive little attention, since most schools of social work provide no discrete ethics courses. Black, Hartley, Kirk-Sharp, and Whelley (1989) discovered that 90 percent of graduate schools of social work surveyed offered no courses in ethics. Where ethics are taught through discrete courses or infusion in others, emphasis is primarily on direct practice, not consultation.

Community mental health centers, once a major provider of consultation, offer little continuing education on ethics to their staff. A recent survey of centers in Colorado revealed that only an average of 1.27 hours were devoted to ethics training during the year prior to the survey (Handelsman, 1989, p. 42). Time assigned specifically to consultation ethics is not mentioned at all.

The NASW code of ethics is described by Reamer (1987, p. 188) as an important "symbolic document" but not one providing precise, unequivocal guidelines for the practitioner. The code provides even less guidance for the consultant, whose ethical decisions are often more complicated than those in direct practice. The NASW code, therefore, although a useful philosophical base, must be extended and made explicit for application in consultation practice.

Current trends suggest that the number of consultants in private practice will increase in the coming years, so the area of ethics in consultation practice needs serious attention. Private consultation by even the most competent persons presents special ethical risks because the protections of agency policy are usually lacking.

Caution and self-discipline on the part of the consultant are also essential because consultee organizations and their staffs are often unsophisticated in evaluating consultant competence. Similarly, consumers usually lack the training and skills to evaluate the consultant's performance. Therefore, sensitivity to ethical questions is often a primary responsibility of the consultant.

Currently in education for consultation it is important to recognize the possibility of some influences of the national "climate" of the 1980s on students' choice of consultation as a specialization. This "climate" includes a heavy emphasis on personal and corporate financial gain, deregulation of numerous operations, and widespread unethical behavior of individuals and organizations in high places. Just one example is James Watt, former director of the Department of Interior, who charged a $300,000 "consultation" fee for a few telephone calls on a HUD contract (Cotton, 1989, p. 2B). Some students view consultation as a high-status, "trendy" form of private practice that produces large fees without regulation. Some view it as a form of practice they can enter quickly after graduation, unmindful of the necessity for development of direct practice competence.

As agents of change, consultants are confronted with "the critical ethical issue: what right does anyone have to try to change the behavior of anyone else?" (Dyer, 1986, p. 280). Dyer adds that in the fifteen years of the Master's program in Organizational Behavior at Brigham Young University the biggest problems were with students' unethical behaviors. The preparation of a consultant, he maintains, should include "helping those who enter this profession to understand the ethical concerns, and to be prepared to face them ethically."

Personal and professional ethics of academically based consultants present special demands associated with contracts, amount of time spent in consultation for private gain, "borrowing" university resources and reputation for consultation purposes, confidentiality, and other issues. Payne and Desman (1987, p. 106) point up dangers in taking ethical risks that may "besmirch the reputation of the university and faculty colleagues."

Although this chapter is not intended as an ethics "primer," it is designed to alert students, teachers, practitioners, and consumers of consultation to critical phases of the consultation process in which there are possibilities for unethical behavior. Such dangers exist because of inadequate preparation for consultation by consultant and consultee, or because of consultants' manipulation of the practice for personal gain. These phases are (1) exploration of the invitation with the consultee organization, (2) formulation of a working contract, (3) consultation in action (operations), (4) evaluation of consultation process and outcomes, and (5) closure of consultation operations.

EXPLORATION

When the invitation comes for consultation, whether from within the organization or from an outside source, a basic question for both consultee and consultant is, "Is this a right fit?" "Fit" considerations include working compatibility and philosophy and mission of consultee and the consultant organization. Can they work together openly and with some degree of satisfaction? Are they comfortable enough in the relationship to work effectively? Is there sufficient agreement on personal and professional values as they relate to the purpose of the consultation and to the consultant's role? Perceptions of this role may change as consultation progresses and may need to be reexamined.

A second crucial question before entry into contract negotiations concerns clarity of purpose of the contemplated consultation. Is the purpose clearly understood by both parties and are both parties entering into the relationship for the same reasons? Sometimes differences in this area may not be apparent in the exploration phase, after completion of a contract, or even after consultation operations have continued for some time.

Such a difference is illustrated in my experience with a public health nursing staff, described in Chapter 5. The public health nurse director, although fully recognizing and supportive of the importance of public health nursing services to the mental health of their patients, was at first perhaps even more concerned about communications problems among her staff which were affecting work morale. The health department physician director also viewed the morale problem as detrimental to work efficiency. Both saw the mental health consultant as someone who might help with these problems but may have valued him less, in the early work together, as one who could strengthen the mental health components of the nurses' work with their patients.

The consultant, not fully aware of their motivations regarding his presence, justified his work on the basis of the nurses' contributions to the mental health aspects of their work as part of their total efforts. The difference in motivations of the several parties began to surface as changes in work methods were sought to increase consultation effectiveness. Through frank discussion at all levels, satisfactory solutions were achieved so that the several goals, although never totally incompatible, could be reconciled in work objectives and methods.

The potential professional and ethical dilemma in this example became apparent when the differences in purposes of consultation were recognized. The solution to the dilemma was effected through candid discussion of differences and a resolution of them through some changes in the consultation process. The changes addressed the several problems in ways that were still consistent with the mental health goals that had brought the consultant there.

Consultant and consumer assessment of the provider's competence for the consultation task is of critical importance before any contract is considered. The statement by Keith-Lucas (1977, p. 351), "The obligation to practice within one's own knowledge and skill is a clear professional responsibility," was made in regard to direct practice but has an obvious application to consultation. Competency assessment may not be made in depth, however, before fitness for the consultation role and clarity of consultation purposes are first fully considered.

Competency assessment for the particular task in question rests heavily on the consultant's shoulders. Among the reasons for this is the fact that consumers frequently lack training for evaluating consultant qualifications and further may regard the consultant as omnipotent. Also, since ethical violations in this (and other) areas are likely to go unnoticed, the consultant must exercise self-discipline in competence assessment. Snow and Gersick (1986, p. 393) point out: "Unless a client is aware that a particular action violates ethical standards, chooses to do something about the action, and knows what to do about it, the behavior will go unnoticed to the outside world."

CONTRACT

The contract, or "statement of understanding," if properly conceived by responsible parties, must be an ethical document inherently concerned with the value and quality of the relationship as well as the conditions for the association. Working details of the contract and its ethical implications were presented in Chapter 4. Here we will merely highlight certain aspects that carry special dangers for neglect or abuse of ethical considerations. During the exploratory phase, details for a proposed consultant–consultee working relationship may have been delegated to agency supervisory, service, or community personnel who are to be directly involved in the consultation process and affected by its outcomes. At the point of contract negotiations, however, administrative or executive staff must be actively engaged, not only to ensure suitable financial arrangements and effective working processes but also to confirm a philosophical and psychological "fit" regarding missions. Gallessich (1982, p. 400) admonishes consultants "to enter an agency through the express permission of its executive officer" and to ascertain that consultant services "are relevant to and consistent with the organization's needs and goals."

The contract should provide for periodic review and changes in consultation focus, working arrangements or involvement of significant new parties if such should be necessary. Even with the most thorough exploration before consultation, there are often circumstances, events, and relationships that cannot be predicted during exploration or that change during consultation, necessitating alterations in emphasis and direction.

Requirements for confidentiality (to be discussed later in the chapter), essential as they are, must be selective enough to protect persons and organizations from harm if possible danger becomes apparent to either of the contracting parties. Flexibility in confidentiality assurances may also be indicated if questionable professional practices, funding irregularities, distortion of data, or other unethical behavior by the consultee become apparent to the consultant and are in direct conflict with her or his value system.

Proper safeguards for confidentiality that also allow professional fleximobility in certain circumstances are summarized in the Hippocratic oath: "whatever things I see or hear concerning the life of men in the attendance on the sick or even apart therefrom, which ought not to be noised abroad, I will keep silence thereon, counting such things to be as sacred secrets."

The contract offers opportunity beyond the exploration phase for further reality testing by the consultant of his or her competence for the task. In this final step before the process begins, additional insights may come through disciplined self-appraisal as the consultant examines again, "Am I entering into this contract because I really think I can fulfill its expectations, or is my motivation centered primarily on a desire for power over others, self-enrichment, or a need to be liked?"

OPERATIONS

Professional ethics requires consultation to be carried out in accordance with the contract guidelines. These cover agreements on such matters as consultation objectives, time for individual sessions and the total process, size and composition of the consultee audience, use of case materials in sessions, and confidentiality.

Thorough as the exploratory and contract negotiations may be in the discussion and development stages, unanticipated problems are certain to develop or subtle factors may be found to have been overlooked. Two examples are ideological or values conflicts that emerge during operations, and an expectation that a consultant will provide supervisory and administrative personnel with information for use in staff evaluation. Some case illustrations from my own experience will serve to describe such dilemmas in consultation practice.

In the first case, an ideological value conflict emerged between the consultant (myself) and a representative of a consultee committee working together to develop a community mental health service.

The exploration and contract stages had been successfully completed, and the conflict did not surface until after consultation was well into the operational phase and there had been substantial progress toward the mutually agreed upon objectives of developing a Family Guidance and Consultation Service to offer counseling, community consultation, education, and organization services under the administration of a city–county public health department.

One influential and highly effective member of a community steering committee suggested that since the proposed service would at first have to operate on very limited funds and would be highly experimental, the counseling recipients should be restricted to *whites*, at least for the first few years of operation. This committee member was highly respected in the community and had consistently provided good leadership in the prevention and modification of problems. His continued work on the committee was crucial for achievement of goals. The response to his suggestion could have been critical in the consultant's relationship with both him and the committee as a whole and might have signaled the end of the consultant's work with them.

Although there was no question in my mind about the position I would take, the response was a carefully measured and gentle one. I first reviewed some of the organizational process up to that point and some of the survey data regarding needs for services. Then I said that I could not continue with a process that would deny services to anyone who needed them. If such a position should be unacceptable to him or others on the committee, they would be free to proceed on their own or seek consultation from other sources.

The response was not contested. Had it been, I would have urged discussion with the full committee, and others as needed, to ensure freedom of access for all to a needed public service.

A second case, from my work with public health nurses (Chapter 5), tested operational ethics. As part of the exploratory process, the consultant asked to accompany some of the nurses, on a strictly voluntary basis, on home visits, observe in maternal and child health clinics, and sit in on interagency conferences and selected intraagency staff sessions. It is important to mention that in the group and individual mental health conferences to follow with the consultant, supervisory and administrative personnel usually participated with the staff nurses.

From these several exposures to nurses' work, supervisory and administrative personnel on a number of occasions asked the consultant to give evaluative impressions of the nurses' performance, sometimes in order to help them make decisions about nurses' promotions or even termination. The consultant had to remind them that this was not a part of the agreed-upon purposes of consultation and that such violations of confidentiality and purpose would seriously damage and might even destroy working relationships with staff at all levels. Furthermore, the consultant explained, the fact that he was a social worker and not a nurse prohibited his evaluation of their performance as public health nurses.

I have experienced similar testing of operational ethics in consultation work with Head Start, Community Action, public school staffs, clergymen, and other personnel through requests for evaluative content. Although the circumstances were different with each group, my responses were consistent.

Persons suffering with emotional problems, often with family disturbances as well, are frequently involved with a variety of community agency services, such as welfare, school, hospital, and law enforcement. Unfortunately each service often operates independently or without knowledge of another's operation. Some services may in fact be working in direct opposition to what others are doing (Rieman, 1983). Mental health consultation must often help focus on the importance of coordinated interagency efforts. Doing so requires time and skill on the part of service providers. It also raises confidentiality issues in consultation with them. These can be dealt with professionally and ethically if there is real commitment to the need for coordinated approaches to make services effective.

The time involved and complexity of such efforts, plus concerns about client rights and fears of litigation, sometimes push service providers (and consultants too) to "hide behind confidentiality" for survival purposes. The result is little or no exchange of information within and between agencies. I have found, however, that when the need is presented properly by service staff, most clients and patients will encourage such exchange. "Helping with the hurt" is usually more important to them than "who knows about my problem."

As consultation progresses and consultees become increasingly comfortable in the relationship, they sometimes reveal more than is necessary or appropriate about themselves, clients, or agencies. Consultants need to be alert to possible violation of confidentiality and ethics and intervene when such is indicated.

The consultant, too, out of curiosity may be tempted to press for information that has little or no relevance to the problem at hand. Payne and Desman (1987, p. 105) speak well to this and related issues of confidentially: ". . . there is a fine line between *the need to know* and *voyeurism,* between *organizational necessity* and *respect for personal privacy,* between the *practical use* and the *self serving abuse* of information."

Still another ethical risk in consultation, especially for consultants with extensive backgrounds in clinical practice, is to allow or even encourage a consultation relationship to slip into a therapeutic one in which there may be considerably more comfort than in the newer and less well-defined consultation role. Gallessich (1982, pp. 105, 387) states that mental health consultants, in particular, tend to draw consultants into "dependent or 'sick' roles." She also describes a related problem of consultants—the "law of the hammer," which holds that they look at problems in terms of their particular skills: "to a person with a hammer, everything looks like a nail."

The mental health consultant is engaged to help with work problems, not personal ones. Yet the very nature of problems discussed in consultation invariably stimulates the injection of personal problems. The line between them is sometimes thin, but the discerning consultant will see the differences and also the danger (such as transference) of allowing the relationship to focus on personal rather than work problems. The discerning and ethical consultant will also take necessary corrective action in such a way as not to embarrass the consultee or jeopardize the consultant relationship.

Group consultation sessions present other special dangers when personal problems are injected. For example, the immediate comfort or stimulation of the consultee in introducing a personal problem to the consultant may later turn to discomfort with staff colleagues. Such intimate disclosures by the consultee may even result in more serious problems of work relationships with colleagues or supervisory or administrative personnel who may be present in the group session.

Caplan (1970, p. 26) introduces another danger of injecting personal problems into consultation. It may result in lowered work productivity, whereas a primary goal of consultation is increasing work effectiveness. Caplan also describes how the consultee, because of feelings of trust and respect for the consultant, may try to utilize the consultant for personal help, thereby changing the relationship from a coordinate one to a superior–subordinate one as in psychotherapy.

The range and complexity of problems confronted in consultation are tremendous, particularly when consultation is provided over an extended period of time. This diversity of problems sometimes requires bringing in supplementary assistance, or even replacing skills provided by the primary consultant. Competencies different from those of the consultant may be indicated from others in varied roles such as educator, interpreter, organizer, or consultant from another specialized area.

In one case, after a careful self-study of needs for human services, the community discovered that several agencies had high priorities and the addition of any one of them to the community would be a positive development. These included child welfare, probation, public health, and mental health. The consultant, although reasonably well informed about all of these services, decided that the community steering committee should have the benefit of specialists in each of these areas in addition to his own (social work–mental health) before deciding which services they would support at this stage, and in what order. It was believed that bringing in consultation experts from other fields would help ensure objective decisions about new services and their priorities. The mental health consultant did not want his good working relationship with the steering committee to have undue influence on their choice of services, or to risk a possible conflict of interest as a social work representative of a mental health agency.

The consultant suggested sources of expertise in the several fields. When they were selected, he briefed them about the community in such a way as to protect confidentiality. He also made careful efforts to coordinate his work with theirs in the consultation, education, and organization activities. The results of these coordinated endeavors resulted in the almost simultaneous organization of several human services, including a mental health agency that was an administrative part of a city–county health department.

In this case, the consultant was guided largely by his own professional orientation, but he also had the advantage of testing and refining his ethics at crucial points with sensitive and enlightened administrative and staff personnel from his sponsoring organization. Similar ethics testing can be made at strategic points by all consultants through associates, colleagues, or other sources. Private consultants particularly, functioning without the customary protections of agency structure and supervision, might find monitoring useful through ethics committees such as those described by Reamer (1987), or small informal discussion groups of kindred souls similar to those helpful to Seibert and Proctor (1984).

EVALUATION

Evaluation is one of the most neglected aspects of consultation. Ethical considerations in relation to evaluation of consultation services are often overlooked in contract arrangements and subsequent operations.

Ethical neglect, through avoidance of evaluation or failure to use adequate mechanism to measure the consultation process and outcomes, results from a variety of factors. These include inability to recognize the importance of ethics in this phase of operations, insensitivity to the topic, indifference, and manipulation of the subject by consultant or consultee for a number of reasons.

Educators and practitioners should be alerted to some of the issues in evaluation procedures if they are to be carried out in ethical fashion. Each consultation scenario is of course different, and the issues presented in the following questions are broad. They and others must be adapted to each specific consultation operation.

1. Is the purpose of evaluation relevant to consultation objectives, or is it just something carried out to meet grant or other bureaucratic requirements?
2. Does the consultant really believe in the need for evaluation, or does she or he agree to the process primarily to fulfill contract obligations?
3. Is evaluation built into consultation content and process planning, or is it added as an afterthought merely to satisfy certain constituencies?
4. Will evaluation effectively measure outcomes of consultation as outlined in the purposes set forth initially or as revised for valid operational reasons?
5. Does evaluation look at staying within contract agreement boundaries in terms of time, method, audience, confidentiality, consultee sharing of discussion materials, individual and joint responsibilities of consultant and consultee, and other such items?
6. Are there adequate safeguards to ensure objectivity in evaluation design, data collection, and analysis?
7. Is there an effort to appraise actual application of consultation content in the practice work setting, as well as in academic discussion about it in consultation sessions?
8. Is evaluation planned and carried out, informally at least, throughout the consultation process, as well as at the conclusion of the project, to test whether it is meeting needs, or requires alteration to improve effective-

ness? The author has found it to be essential with all consultation audiences (if there is prolonged contact with them or just a few hours) to take frequent "soundings." "How are we doing" questions asked in creative ways elicit invaluable information about how well the consultant and consultee are working together, whether they are accomplishing their goals, or whether content and/or process need to be revised mildly or radically, or whether consultation should be terminated for positive or negative reasons.

TERMINATION

Carefully built relationships and procedures, so essential to the success of consultation, must be "delicately dismantled" (Smith & Corse, 1986, p. 267) as part of the termination process. These authors aptly and succinctly comment on the importance of the task: "Termination creates disequilibrium and often will prove to be the first major test of the resilience of patterns created via the consultation."

In spite of its value and the skills required for this phase of consultation, termination, like evaluation, is an often neglected procedure (Gallessich, 1982, p. 242), both in education and practice. One issue with ethical implications is the creation of unhealthy dependency in the consulter/consultee organization and failure by the consultant to deal with the dependency either earlier or during the critical stages of termination. As a consequence, termination may be avoided or prolonged by both parties—the consultant to maintain power or financial gain, perhaps; the consultee to protect the comfort of having an "expert" close at hand or to avoid personal and professional responsibility for acting independently.

Inherent in ethical closure of a consultation relationship is exploration in a variety of ways about psychological and technical readiness for the consultee to continue practice without the consultant's indirect assistance. Even under the best of circumstances and the absence of unhealthy dependence, the consultee usually needs skilled help in this aspect as part of the termination process.

In my group mental health consultation with public health nurses (Chapter 5), in order to make the process most effective and to begin preparation for termination, at timely points of the operation I requested and increasingly received assistance from the participants for group content and process responsibility. This included leadership in selection of case materials, moderating and recording of discussion, orientation of new members, and observation and evaluation of group process in the consultation sessions. Earlier in the operation the consultant had to assume a major role, for example, in presiding over the sessions in addition to serving as a consultant on discussion content.

As an aid to group development, a workshop organized and staffed by the consultant and his colleagues focused on group process techniques and simulations to prepare them to assume leadership. This workshop and other shifting and sharing of group responsibilities not only contributed significantly to productive sessions with the consultant but also enabled staff to carry on after consultation came to a close.

Following formal evaluation of the consultant's work with the public health nursing staff by an outside specialist (Appendix B), the consultant and staff participated in a series of sessions to discuss the evaluation findings. There was a dual purpose: for immediate integration and application of the evaluation data, and as a further step toward their assuming independence in major group functioning roles. It was also done to help them incorporate mental health components in their work with patients.

Careful internal and external evaluation during critical stages of consultation may reveal that a different kind of consultation, training, or technical assistance is needed than can be provided by the present consultant. Professional/ethical behavior on the consultant's part then would be to help the consultee find competent sources of ongoing help and not to prolong the relationship, even if it has been satisfying for both parties and could be exploited for personal reasons through delay or avoidance of termination.

REFERENCES

Black, P., Hartley, E., Kirk-Sharp, C., & Whelley, J. (1989) Ethics curricula: A national survey of graduate schools of social work. Paper presented at the Council on Social Work Education, Annual Program Meeting, Chicago.

Caplan, G. (1970). *The theory and practice of mental health consultation*. New York: Basic Books.

Cotton, L. (1989, June 27). HUD Mess Rooted In Indifference, *The Evening Sun*, Baltimore, as reprinted in the *St. Louis Dispatch*, Mirror of Public Opinion.

Dyer, W. (1986). Invited commentary: Preparing a new consultant, *Consultation*, 5, 278–283.

Gallessich, J. (1982). *The profession and practice of consultation*. San Francisco: Jossey-Bass.

Handelsman, M. (1989). Ethics training at mental health centers, *Community Mental Health Journal*, 25, 42–50.

Keith-Lucas, A. (1977). Ethics in social work, *Encyclopedia of Social Work* (Vol. 1). Washington, D.C.: National Association of Social Workers.

Payne, S., & Desman, R. (1987). The academician as a consultant. In S. Payne & B. Charnov, *Ethical dilemmas for academic professionals*. Springfield, Ill.: Charles C Thomas.

Reamer, R. (1987). Ethics committees in social work, *Social Work, 32*, 188–172.

Rieman, D. (1983). Strengthening coordination and collaboration procedures among mental health and other community agency workers, *Quality Review Bulletin, Journal of Quality Assurance*, 218–219.

Seibert, D., & Proctor, W. (1984). *The ethical executive*. New York: Simon & Schuster.

Smith, K., & Corse, S. (1986). The process of consultation: Critical issues. In F. Mannino, E. Trickett, M. Shore, M. Kidder, and G. Levine (Eds.), *Handbook of mental health consultation*. Rockville, Md.: National Institute of Mental Health, United States Public Health Service.

Snow, D., & Gersick, K. (1986). Ethical and professional issues in mental health consultation. In F. Mannino, E. Trickett, M. Shore, M. Kidder, & G. Levin (Eds.), *Handbook of mental health consultation*. Rockville, Md. National Institute of Mental Health, United States Public Health Service.

CHAPTER 8

Maintenance and Extension of Consultation Services, Knowledge, and Skills

Iscoe (1983), in a commentary on D'Augelli's work (1982), said it points out that consultation is no longer the glamour issue of community mental health centers. In terms of social policy, consultation remains a basically nonreimbursable expense. Until this situation is changed or recipient organizations are willing to budget for *ongoing* consultations, the future of consultation is not a bright one.

The full impact of current federal policy (or lack of it) regarding health, mental health, and other human services, along with reductions of financial support, will not be fully known for some time. We do know, however, that social, economic, health, and mental health problems are on the increase. Thus mental health and other human services programs and staffs are forced to "do more with less." Whether this can be accomplished is debatable, but with the reduction of supports and increases in problems, the argument for not only maintaining consultation activities but expanding them becomes even stronger because of its multiplier effects.

Unfortunately, consultation services as described in the Texas study (Chapter 5), for example, have been sharply curtailed. This cutback creates a triple danger: (1) loss of important services, (2) diminution (through disuse) of hard-won consultation knowledge and skills gained over the past several decades, (3) threats to educational preparation for consultation.

In further defense of consultation as an important preventative, Justice (1982) brings clarity in definition of prevention and also illustrates through examples that it does work and can be measured. He carefully points out differences between preventing major psychoses and the lesser kinds of problems of living brought to mental health centers, such as self-defeating behaviors and relationship disturbances. Justice cites several successful examples of primary prevention, including (1) Broussard's work with high-risk infants (First Born Preventive Intervention Program in Pittsburgh, 1977), (2) Spivack and Shure's 1977 work with low-income children to increase coping skills and prevent behavioral problems, and (3) Silverman's 1972 work with newly widowed persons and the beneficial effects of widow-to-widow programs.

Among those who insist that primary prevention is fantasy, Justice (p. 223) explains, are the "many professionals whose livelihood and status" are dependent largely on treatment and who do not welcome the idea of prevention.

Hollister (1982, p. 232) explains that preventive efforts have been slowed by "professional scoffing, the acute need to focus resources on the very ill, and by premature demands that prevention prove itself before it has had a chance to mature its technologies to prevent multietiological disorders." In contrast, he points out, "we gave psychotherapy 40 years to mature before insisting it be evaluated. As a result, prevention has received only desultory support at the governmental and professional level." He adds that preventive technology is maturing "by first learning how to meet limited goals, leaving the prevention of the major disabilities until later, just as prevention in physical medicine has done."

As I described earlier in the book, where there is a commitment to prevention as a central part of community mental health programs, ways are found not only to maintain consultation at previous levels but actually to increase it. It is a matter of policy, but current policy in many centers and state programs discourages consultation and reduces it to a low-volume activity.

How such policy can be changed and proper political strategies developed to encourage the funding of consultation is indeed a difficult problem, but one that must be met if we are to avoid regression to pre-Kennedy and earlier days of prevention neglect. Someone has said that mental health programs and approaches advance and regress in about twenty-year cycles. It would be tragic indeed if we have to wait another twenty years before consultation is again regarded as an invaluable activity and appropriately funded along with direct services.

CONTINUING EDUCATION

Continuing education efforts are an important way to improve provision and use of consultation, influence policy decisions, and help maintain and expand consultation activities. There has been impressive growth in the design, volume, and quality in continuing education in consultation and related activities. Improvements in content and method have been greater, I believe, than in basic education, where there is more "locking in" by tradition and there are fewer pressures for redesign. However, many graduate programs in social work, described in the next chapter, give inadequate attention to consultation. Smith

(1975) discovered that only 15 of 50 schools of social work surveyed offered a course or workshop on consultation as part of their continuing education programs.

To illustrate that continuing education can improve skills in both provision and use of consultation I cite an example close at hand. I directed an NIMH-funded, three-year continuing education project for mental health and other community agency professionals in Missouri (Ehrlich, Rieman, Stretch, 1973). It was a multidisciplinary project on three interrelated themes: mental health consultation, community organization, and coordination skills and services development. Actual educational activities were limited to eighteen months because of the time required for staff recruitment, participant registration, research design, research analysis, and write-up of the final report.

Sixty mental health and 26 personnel from community agencies participated, including social workers (the majority), nurses, psychiatrists, psychologists, clergy, and some in related disciplines. Facilities represented in this experimental project were two state hospitals, one rural and one urban; one urban community mental health center; and a variety of community agencies including public health, welfare, education, social service, legal aid, regional planning, and community action.

Educational method included two major workshops (two to four days) fifteen months apart, and twelve monthly seminars at each of the three participating mental health facilities for a total of 36. Composition of the seminar groups included mental health personnel from each facility and representatives of community agencies in the three catchment areas (east and southeast Missouri).

Major educational content consisted of theoretical material and applications, selected field experiences presented for discussion and analysis, and simulation games.

Research evaluation focused on changes in participants' knowledge, attitudes, skills, and interagency activities in relation to the major project themes. Pre- and post-project measures were made. All of the research conclusions were data based. In the summary of major findings, Stretch, the research consultant (Ehrlich, Rieman & Stretch, 1973) states:

> Considering the variety of independent data generated in attempting to measure the project's overall effect and impact as well as the several subanalyses which produced consistently corroborative data, the overwhelming conclusion points to the general success of the project. It also attests to the differential effect and impact associated with programmed mix of professional, institutional and community characteristics.
>
> The general degree of project effectiveness, the project's specific utility, and current and future applications are very heartening. It is hoped that the project has not only proven useful in the here and now, but that it will have proven in the long run to have been a catalytic agent for the continued upgrading of services and increased excellence in community mental health practices. (p. 82).

Representative of what administrators of participating agencies thought about the project is this statement by a director of a mental health center:

> In the area of specific agency or departmental responsibilities the agency responsibility was changed [by the project] from a narrow view of treating the mentally ill who came to the agency to improving the mental health of a community population located in a defined geographic area. The responsibility was seen as extending along a time continuum, so that patients had a treatment career, employees had a career ladder, high-risk groups needed prevention measures designed, positive action of civil rights was related to mental health delivery, and black studies were needed to understand patients' actions and communications.
>
> In the area of overall agency mission, the mission was changed from the right to treatment to the right of mental health. (p. 87)

Following are some impressions of the project by the Director of Community Mental Health, Missouri Division of Mental Health (Cravens, 1973):

> . . . It often happens that staffs, if presented with the opportunity, will outgrow the administration. This results in the often heard cry that a supervisor will not allow a staff member to exercise a new skill or take on a different responsibility. It then follows that staff development for supervisory personnel becomes a key to institutional change. This project had as several goals the offering of new information, development of previously unavailable skills, and the construction of a philosophy of service. Coupled with these objectives was the involvement of upper management in the training activities.
>
> During the final phase of the project, the Division of Mental Health is now taking an active step forward to reduce the state hospital population by a significant degree. This effort will require knowledge of community organizations, an awareness of placement settings, familiarity with resources for service in the community, and well-established consultation skills.
>
> . . . This project represents the first step, taken some time ago, in making possible revolutionary changes that are about to take place in Division programming. Although the changes could be mandated, they could not be maximized without staff development. The project has permitted, in some cases, for the participants to discover the uniqueness of each community and to see more relevant ways for the hospital to serve the community.
>
> The project has also suggested the need for staff development to be planned, ongoing, and directed toward the many working levels of a hospital employee. It is also through staff development that techniques become refined, programs assessed, and services to people improved. The results of this project will not, like the printed report, be filed on a dusty bookshelf. The impact has been felt by each project participant and, to varying degrees, each participant was changed with the change reflected in work performed. The impact is timely because it is through new-found knowledge and ability that significant modifications in Division programs will be possible. (pp. 209–210)

Goldmeier and Mannino (1986) commented about the evaluation of this continuing education project and its impact on consultees and their services as follows (italics added):

Unfortunately, special courses and educational programs in consultation generally provide little or no information that can be used to judge their success or failure, i.e., their effect on those who completed them. Programs that do try to evaluate their training efforts often show positive results but tend to focus primarily on the reactive level. Because of this, most programs fail to show that training in consultation improves the quality or impact of consultation in services. *An exception to this was an evaluation carried out at the University of Missouri School of Social Work of a continuing education project in mental health consultation and community organization from 1970 to 1973.* Using sophisticated "pre-post" methodology and some rather unique measuring instruments, the evaluation clearly showed that the training project significantly increased the participants' range and degree of knowledge concerning mental health consultation, and the amount of time spent in work with the community (solid evidence of program impact). A change in attitudes towards consultation and some amount of skill development were also shown, but not as markedly. *This evaluation is unique in social work, if not in the broader mental health field in general, in being able to offer data-based conclusions, demonstrating that training can be effective in increasing the impact of mental health consultation services.* (pp. 187–188)

As a result of the success of this continuing education project, the director for community mental health and I had a series of conferences with directors, chiefs of services, board members, and others from four community mental health centers in the Kansas City area. One of the highest priority needs on which there was unanimous agreement was for strengthening (through continuing education) professional staff–board collaboration in program design, implementation, interpretation, and funding. Funds were secured from NIMH, and a second three-year continuing education project was carried out, involving more than 200 board and staff members from twenty-four Missouri mental health facilities. The multidisciplinary effort was designed and programmed to strengthen staff–board efforts in program-planning and decision-making processes such as those regarding proper balances of direct and indirect services, quality of life priorities, and mental health–environmental issues.

Maximum utilization was made of participant-directed learning in a carefully planned, supervised, and continuously appraised series of workshops, seminars, and field practice experiences totaling almost 14,000 contact hours.

Rigorous evaluation by an independent research team, Bowman and Neff, utilizing pre- and post-project questionnaires and interview data, revealed the following: ". . . the evidence indicates that the project had a favorable impact on the collaboration of board and staff, on overall functioning of board and staff, and on their attitudes toward community mental health" (Rieman, Currall, Bowman, & Neff, 1979, p. 187).

Although these projects were extended continuing education efforts, with NIMH funding, the methods used and content can be replicated in other places, at local, state, and regional levels. If there are insufficient agency or individual resources, peer consultation offers one solution to improving worker and agency skills and programs in these and related items. The worth and conduct of peer consultation are described by Chaiklin and Munson (1983). Peer consultation as a method of training can be carried out, they report, with or without a leader if there is proper motivation and competence within the group. It can also be carried out with minimal expense, since the participants can be the teachers or trainers.

Although continuing education efforts have improved greatly during the past several decades, there is still tremendous room for improvement and extension of training. All too often when one attends a conference or workshop on consultation, leaders provide little more than warmed-over versions of Caplan's theories and methods. Although these are tremendous contributions to the field, there have been many important refinements by numerous practitioners and teachers of consultation in recent years.

We are also now at the point, certainly, where training institutes can be highly specialized and beamed at homogeneous audiences with specific consultation interests. This does not mean that "waterfront" approaches have not been useful, but we are at a juncture where content and method can and should be adapted to specific audiences, in terms of, for example, special areas of interest or length and depth of consultation.

State departments of health, welfare, mental health, mental retardation, and education, as well as professional organizations from the several disciplines, should provide or encourage enriched in-service training opportunities aimed at consultant practitioners, consumers of consultation, and lay and professional leaders. Special emphasis should be given to the requirement for specialized knowledge and techniques necessary for providing "consultation for consultants." This will be discussed in Chapter 10.

Through continuing education and on-the-job efforts, personnel in clinic, family agency, and similar settings can be encouraged to initiate or extend their consultation efforts through *case collaboration–consultation*. Such specialized personnel may have some direct contact with patients and clients in collaboration with less specialized personnel, for demonstration of service methods or for diagnostic or other purposes. Following these usually time-limited contacts, the specialized staff may withdraw from direct contact with the client, but continue in a consultant role with the less specialized staff. The first (direct) phase is really collaboration, not consultation, but it is one way of getting into consultation and can be a cost-saving activity.

Case collaboration–consultation is closer to traditional practice and therefore may be a good starting-off point for many. If the skills of care-givers can be developed, mental health center and other personnel can shorten their contact but still provide ongoing help to those who assume case responsibility. If the work of care-givers is strengthened in this way, referrals can be more selective to mental health and other specialized facilities, and services can be extended to larger numbers of people.

If mental health center and other professional helping personnel can begin to "let go" earlier, they may also develop interest in extending their skills and activities in "pure" types of consultation, in giving assistance to care-giver groups around problems of clients who have no direct contact with the center or other service.

Glasscote, Sussex, Cumming, and Smith (1969, p. 27) reported, in a survey of personnel from agencies using mental health center services (particularly those from the schools and courts), that the personnel preferred treatment services rather than case or program consultation. This finding is not surprising. Many consultants have learned that until agencies and practitioners have had considerable satisfactory help through consultation services, they prefer to shift the case responsibility to the mental health facility or some other specialized service. With support and strengthening of their own helping skills, however, many care-givers find that they can provide a great deal of help to troubled people and in many instances do not need to make a referral to a mental health facility. In the process they also experience considerable satisfaction and are frequently motivated to continue carrying some responsibility for the case rather than referring it to a mental health facility.

The NASW "*Position Statement on Community Mental Health*," although written in 1969, is still timely in presenting further evidence of the need for attention in continuing education for provision and use of consultation. A few excerpts from this report follow (italics added):

> *Consultation, coordination, education, program development, team leadership, social action, are all vital activities which require a strong base and firm value stance. All mental health practitioners need to develop a commitment to utilize indirect services or delivery of services via intermediaries.* Since people are inclined to do what they have been trained to do and feel competent doing, it is not surprising that many experienced practitioners hesitate to change their forms of practice. If mental health personnel are expected to use new skills, *continuing education programs must be provided to assure competent practice of these new skills.* Because continuing education programs often reach people in leadership positions who influence the practice of others, they may be among the most effective vehicles for rebuilding the ideologies and technologies of our mental health program. . .
>
> . . . the shortage of mental health personnel should be dealt with as a matter of *utilization* as well as a matter of helpers. While making a maximum effort to increase the numbers of mental health professionals, graduate education,

continuing education, and in-service training programs must be modified to help practitioners produce maximum impact in the community. Social action, program planning, coordination, consultation, and other forms of indirect service will greatly enhance the social utility of mental health professionals. (pp. 7; 10)

REFERENCES

Chaiklin, H., & Munson, C. (1983, Summer). Peer consultation in social work, *The Clinical Supervisor, 1*(2), 24–25.

Cravens, R. (1973). Implications. In P. Ehrlich, D. Rieman, & J. Stretch, *Development, extension and utilization of mental health consultation, community organization and coordination skills and services.* University of Missouri–Columbia, Social Work Extension Program and Missouri Division of Mental Health (Grant No. NIMH 5T515 MH 12444).

D'Augelli, A. (1982, Summer). A funny thing happened on the way to the community: Consultation and education in community mental health centers, or how I learned to stop worrying about prevention and love third-party payments, *Journal of Prevention, 2*(4).

Ehrlich, P., Rieman, D., & Stretch, J. (1973). *Development, extension and utilization of mental health consultation, community organization and coordination skills and services.* University of Missouri–Columbia, Social Work Extension Program and Missouri Division of Mental Health (Grant No. NIMH 5T515 MH 12444).

Glasscote, R., Sussex, J., Cumming, E., & Smith, L. (1969) *Community mental health centers—An interim appraisal.* Washington, D.C.: The Joint Information Service of American Psychiatric Association.

Goldmeier, J., & Mannino, F. (1986). The role of social work in consultation. In F. Mannino, E. Trickett, M. Shore, M. Kidder, & G. Levin (Eds.), *Handbook of mental health consultation.* Rockville, Md.: National Institute of Mental Health.

Hollister, W. (1982). Evolving strategies. In M. Wagenfeld, P. Lemkau, & B. Justice (Eds.), *Public mental health: Perspectives and prospects.* Beverly Hills, Calif.: Sage Publications.

Iscoe, I. (1983). *Mental health consultation and education.* Unpublished manuscript, University of Texas–Austin.

Justice, B. (1982). Primary prevention—Fact or fantasy. In M. Wagenfeld, P. Lemkau, & B. Justice (Eds.), *Public mental health: Perspectives and prospects.* (pp. 209–226) Beverly Hills, Calif.: Sage Publications.

National Association of Social Workers, Council on Mental Health and Psychiatric Services. (1969, January). *Position statement on community mental health,* pp. 7, 10.

Rieman, D., Currall, J., Jr., Bowman, P., & Neff, F. (1979). *Staff board collaboration in community mental health programs.* University of Missouri–Columbia, Social Work Extension Program and Missouri Department of Mental Health (Grant No. NIMH 5T515 14092) pp. 186–187.

Smith, J. M. B. (1975). Curriculum content course model, *Social work consultation: Implications for social work education.* Doctoral dissertation, University of Utah, pp. 159–169.

CHAPTER 9

Education for Consultation: Refining and Enlarging the Effort

In preparation for writing this book, I contacted the Division of Standards and Accreditation of the Council on Social Work Education, an accrediting organization for the teaching of social work, and requested their help in locating good graduate programs that include consultation theory and methods that I might study. The Council responded that they could not be of much help because "consultation as a part of the masters' curriculum is rarely identified in self-study materials for accreditation." The Council's publication "*Summary Information on Accredited Graduate Social Work Programs,* 1982" also did not provide the needed information. A quick overview of bulletins of schools of social work with accredited Master's programs (92 in 1983)* revealed a rather low number of courses with consultation content, either as a course in itself or as part of another course. In a sizable number of schools consultation content could not be identified at all, and some that had had such content in the past had apparently eliminated it.

I wrote to nine deans of schools that did have some consultation content, requesting information about their courses on consultation, and I received a reply

Material for this chapter was adapted from a paper I presented, "*Consultation—An Undertaught Subject: Recommendations for Strengthening Teaching of This Subject,*" at the annual program meeting, Council on Social Work Education, Miami, March 1986.

*Although this overview was conducted in 1983, my impression is that the current status of consultation teaching remains much the same. There may be even fewer offerings on the subject now, and presented often as a secondary topic in combination with other forms of practice such as social work supervision, administration, or direct services.

from only one. Poor timing may have been one factor: my letter was written not long before the close of the school term, a very busy time for all faculty. Nevertheless, the lack of response may be a clue about the "current state of the art," an indication that in education, as in practice, consultation has suffered a decline.

I was successful in contacting the Graduate School of Social Work, the University of Utah, Salt Lake City, and Dean Eunice O. Shatz put me in touch with two instructors of consultation, Dr. Phyllis Southwick and Dr. Joanne Smith, whom I ultimately interviewed.

At about the same time, I discovered an abstract and course prospectus which Dr. Smith had prepared as part of her doctoral dissertation (1975). Some excerpts will be presented here; they are particularly important and timely for refining and enlarging consultation educational efforts.

The dissertation was an exploratory study with a threefold focus:

1. Identifying the knowledge and skills essential to the practice of social work consultation
2. Determining the nature and degree of social work consultation practiced by a specific group of social workers and what preparation they had for this
3. Describing existing educational efforts in consultation and recommendations for curriculum development and teaching of consultation

The study population consisted of 48 graduates (90.6%) of the Graduate School of Social Work at the University of Utah, class of 1965. The largest number were employed in mental health settings and the next highest in services for children. Seventy-five percent reported having had experience as consultants in their work since graduation. This was in a multiplicity of areas, including program planning, diagnostic evaluation, group work, community organization, program evaluation, and administration.

One of the many striking findings from this study, and one that highlights the importance of education for consultation, was that none of the population could recall content relating specifically to consultation during their MSW program. About 20 percent had had some formal preparation for the role through in-service training programs, workshops, NASW institutes, and other activities.

All reported that consultation should be taught in the MSW and/or continuing education program. Most reported also that a practicum in addition to class offerings would be "ideal." Their responses were quite similar to those in the Texas study (Chapter 6) concerning the importance of teaching consultation during graduate study and some helpful methods for presenting content and skills training.

The second portion of Dr. Smith's study, concerned with existing education for consultation, had a response from 50 deans of 80 graduate schools. Sixteen percent said that no content on consultation was identifiable in their curriculum.

In fifteen schools content was "ambiguous." Examples: "It's in all the practice classes"; "We hit it in Administration I and Administration II and also in the policy planning courses"; "I give it at least an hour in every casework course."

Of the 50 schools responding, only fifteen offered a course or workshop specifically on consultation as part of the continuing education program. Some were planning such programs, but 30 (60%) were not anticipating such offerings.

Dr. Smith expressed concern that a large number of schools have not clarified the content on consultation, nor have they developed a specific course on the subject. She also expressed concern about the limited number of continuing education offerings on the subject.

As part of her doctoral study, Dr. Smith developed a *Curriculum Content Course Model on Social Work Consultation*. With refinements and updating, this was taught as a separate course until recently, when it was combined with a course on Supervision and Consultation. The reason for this change was not clear to me, but apparently it was a combination of budgetary and administrative considerations and student needs, which apparently had become more "clinical."

The original model was designed for doctoral and selected second-year MSW students and for post-MSW practitioners. It consists of the following nine units, each with distinct objectives, learning experiences, and reading assignments.

1. Introduction to Consultation
2. Consultee Systems and Their Needs
3. Overview of the Consultation Process
4. Preparatory Stage
5. Entry Stage
6. Formal Interaction Stage
7. Formal Interaction Stage (continued)
8. Evaluation Stage
9. Termination Stage

The combined course, Supervision and Consultation: Two Leadership Roles in Social Work, consisted of three major units, each with special objectives, learning experiences, and readings: (1) introduction, covering historical development and definitions; (2) change process and its basic elements, covering leadership roles in the change process and the nature of the change process; (3) the functions of supervision and consultation, covering the role of administrative function in supervision and in the consultation process, the role of education in supervision and consultation, the role of enabler/facilitator, and the role of evaluation in supervision and consultation.

The course was taught by Smith and Southwick in nine weekly two-hour classes. Equal time was given to supervision and consultation. It was an elective, but both Southwick and Smith thought it should be a required course. The course was offered to both part-time and full-time students. About 20 percent of full-time students and 50 percent of the part-time students were enrolled in it. The instructors stated that when consultation is taught to a mixture of full-time students and part-time students who are currently in practice, the experience is particularly stimulating and enriching. Role play was extensively used. There was not much time for teaching skills, however. For the most effective teaching of consultation, Smith believed, class size should be limited to six to eight, but their current number was about twelve.

Two references described by Smith and Southwick as exemplary were *The Client Consultant Handbook* (Bell and Nadler, 1979) and *The Profession and Practice of Consultation* (Gallessich, 1982). Particular reference was made to Gallessich's treatment of ethical considerations, a topic that has received little attention in the literature. Dr. Smith said that confidentiality in consultation is a particularly important problem in states with small populations such as Utah.

Two other courses on supervision and consultation, one at the University of Missouri, School of Social Work, Columbia, and the other at St. Louis University, School of Social Services, are described in Appendix C.

QUESTIONS AND RECOMMENDATIONS
FOR TEACHING CONSULTATION

When should consultation be taught during the graduate sequence, or should it be taught then at all? Must there be a sound base of clinical competence before consultation can be effectively taught? Is some practice experience necessary first, and if so, how much is needed? Is consultation learned best through graduate education, continuing education, on-the-job training, or a combination of these and other methods? Should a practicum experience be offered in consultation during graduate training, and if so when?

The following suggestions about preparation for consultation come as a result of my own practice and teaching in consultation, as well as discussions with other practitioners and faculty, including many mentioned in this book.

Since all practitioners, in any area of specialization, will be consumers of consultation fairly early in professional life, and sometimes during field placements, there should be some exposure to consultation theory and practice during graduate training. In addition, many will be thrust into consultation activities frequently and often early in their careers.

Although consultation is still not a finely honed art, there is now a tremendous amount of information available about the use and practice of consultation, and many knowledgeable people to convey that information. Not enough attention is being given to preparation for consultation at the graduate level, however, and even less on how to select and use consultants. For their own sake, potential consultees should know something about the service, since there are unfortunately many who are posing as consultants but lack appropriate skills. There are some also who are unscrupulous and unethical in their practice.

Potential consultees should be taught to be discerning about the "producer and the product."

These are just a few reasons why all students should have some introduction to consultation practice and use. There should be one required three-hour survey course to introduce the subject, with at least some introduction of skills training. Since the student should have at least some beginning competence in direct service delivery, the course probably should not be taught earlier than the second semester of the first graduate year. Later would be even better, but those who want to go beyond the survey course need the opportunity also to take one or more courses in consultation in the second year.

For those with some work experience, and those who want to specialize in consultation, supervision, or administration, there should be an advanced course (also required) which provides further theory and substantial attention to skills development, both in provision and use of consultation services. Some operational exposure to consultation should be provided during the practicum in the second year. For the student who has had considerable prior experience and a good foundation in direct service provision, most or all of the field experience could be devoted to consultation.

Raber (1982) identified those competencies most critical in developing training programs and/or curriculum for consultation and education. He did a study of a population of sixteen experts in consultation and education and 264 practitioners who were directors of C & E services in all the federally funded community mental health centers in the continental United States. The list is presented in its entirety because (1) it presents in a succinct way what competencies are required to provide and support C & E activities, (2) it suggests significant content that must be taught in introductory and more advanced courses, and (3) it is highly consistent with and supportive of what was said in Chapter 4 about desirable attributes of the consultant, the consultee, and sponsor and consumer systems.*

Consultation

Conceptual Knowledge	*Personal Characteristics*
Knows problem solving processes	Respects confidentiality
Knows consultation theory	Has belief in value of consultation to bring change
Knows differences between supervision/education/consultation	Has good judgment
Knows systems theory	Is willing to begin where client is
Knows management theory	Has respect for consultee and organization
	Has integrity

---

*From R. Raber, *Competency based guidelines for the training and development of consultation and education specialists in community mental health centers*. Doctoral dissertation, Kansas State University, Manhattan, Kans., 1982, 88–89, 93. Reprinted by permission.

Education

Knows community resources

Knows prevention concepts

Knows group dynamics theory

Knows problem-solving processes

Knows community development
   concepts

Knows community organization
   concepts

Knows human service systems

Is aware of social/economic/political
   issues of community

Has belief in prevention and mental
   health promotion

Has ability to work with all kinds of
   people

Is open to collaboration

Has commitment to building
   relationships based on equality and
   trust

Public Information

Knows the function of mass media

Knows public speaking principles

Knows marketing approaches

Knows mental health systems

Knows accurate internal agency
   information

Is articulate

Has belief in prevention and mental
   health promotion

Balances accuracy, integrity, popular
   appeal, and attractiveness of person
   and message

Is reliable and dependable

Has intuition/
   ingenuity/creativity/imagination

Management

Knows management theory including:
   budgeting and finance
   staff development
   planning and evaluation
   supervision
   organization
   motivating subordinates
   decision making
   protection of staff
   delegation
   use of authority
   leadership

Knows concepts and theories of C & E

Knows contracting concepts

Knows consultation theory

Knows mental health systems

Is willing to be advocate of C & E
   internally and externally

Is willing to delegate

Is open to feedback

Is open to new methods and ideas

Raber also makes eleven recommendations for further development and teaching of consultation and education. Three are listed here, items 3, 4, and 5 on his list.

- Recommend that the distinctive competencies in the areas of consultation, education, public information, and management be seen as uniquely different, calling for distinctive training strategies.
- Recommend that concepts of ecological change (prevention) be emphasized in the training of C & E specialists allowing for the more adequate integration of prevention, consultation, and education concepts.
- Recommend that the extent of clinical experience not be the determining factor in making judgments concerning the hiring and training of C & E specialists.

I have described minimal amounts and some content for consultation training as applied to graduate social work education. Motivation for more intensive training will come in increasing measure as the professional practices and uses consultation on the job. Although continuing education is still rather minimal and not always sufficiently refined and specialized, there are opportunities for such education through universities, professional organizations, and other sources. Some models, with good potential for replication, were outlined earlier. There seem to be better linkages between continuing education and practice than exist between campus degree programs and practice.

There has been some increase in the volume of graduate courses on consultation offered on a multidiscipline basis, but not enough. Improvement is needed in both the quality and number of such offerings. It is wasteful to offer duplicate courses on one campus when actual differences in content are slight. Courses offered exclusively to one discipline could, with some modification, be addressed to all the mental health professions. The quality of such offerings is also enriched with an interdisciplinary student mix (Rieman, 1982).

HIGHLY CAPSULIZED OFFERINGS

This book has discussed graduate and continuing education in consultation that takes place over an extended period of time. However, sometimes there are only a few hours to introduce the subject. For such circumstances, some experiences and information from guest lectures I have made will be useful.

To make maximum use of very limited time (usually only one or two class sessions of three hours each) I do a brief needs assessment prior to the presentation(s) with a small committee from the class, three to six persons. After some brief getting-acquainted activity, identifying ourselves and our background, and so on, I ask them to help me understand where the class is in its understanding of consultation—the "what," the "why," and the "doing." From this discussion I then seek and make some suggestions as to alternative ways of presenting material to the class and I get their reactions. I ask them also what content they have already had in school or through working experience.

If there is time before the class, I ask them to develop a set of questions that represent their concerns and those of their classmates. I ask each committee member to talk with one or two other students to help frame these questions, and then get them to me a day or two in advance of my presentation(s).

I also distribute brief reading lists for future reference and I make some suggestions about reading materials in advance of the class and explore what kinds of material and in what quantities they would be used.

I also find out about their interest and readiness for role playing a consultation simulation, and whether they prefer to do this as a group of committee members or to involve part or all of the class. We have had numerous kinds of role-playing situations such as individual, client-centered consultation, group consultation, program consultation, and community organization consultation. These have involved from two to twenty members of the class. After completion of the role play we critique it as carefully as time permits.

To suggest role-play content without limiting them (suggestions are meant only to get them thinking), I offer them as possibilities:

- Case problem-working with client
- Staff relationship problem
- Staff–supervisory or administrative problem
- Policy formulation and/or change
- Program planning
- Relationship with another agency or agencies
- Community planning and action about what seems to be a major problem
- Interpretation of an agency to other agencies and/or the general public
- Staff morale–burnout

Also, if there is time, I ask them to give me a brief outline of the role-play situation; short description of the problem, setting, players; the reason why consultation was requested; where the consultant comes from, and so on. If I sense considerable discomfort about class member(s) playing the role of consultant, I offer to be the consultant, at least the first time around.

Content of the formal presentations, in preparation for the role plays, is highly capsulized versions of earlier portions of this book, particularly timeliness of the topic, operational definitions, and sponsors and consumers of consultation.

If there are two sessions, there is a brief introduction to "The How" in the second session. I share some of my consultation experiences, and I ask them to share any they may have had, as either users or providers.

Some examples of questions submitted to me by students in advance of the sessions are the following:

1. Why and how did consultation services originate historically?
2. How are decisions made about the type(s) of consultation to be used?
3. What difference does it make who requests the consultation?

4. How does the consultant get her- or himself invited?

5. What are some ways consultation programs can prove their effectiveness in the face of current financial constraints?

6. Is consultation cost effective?

7. Is consultation being scrapped (provision or use) in some places because of the budget crunch?

8. What are good methods to evaluate consultation?

9. Explain the lack of change in consultation strategies as described in the literature over the past twenty-five years.

10. What if the agency or community doesn't recognize its need for change as might be effected through consultation? Can the consultant be imposed?

The brief, highly concentrated session(s) is, of course, not aimed at skills development but rather is intended to give students an interesting introduction to the subject in the hope that it will, first, stimulate further study on and off the campus, and second, provide some beginning guides to good sources and use of consultants.

REFERENCES

Bell, C. R., and Nadler, L. (Eds.). (1979). *The client consultant handbook*. Houston: Gulf Publishing Company.

Gallessich, J. (1982). *The profession and practice of consultation*. San Francisco: Jossey-Bass.

Raber, R. (1982). *Competency based guidelines for the training and development of consultation and education specialists in community mental health centers*. Doctoral dissertation, Kansas State University, Manhattan, Kans.

Rieman, D. (1982). Changing practices in personnel preparation and use. In M. Wagenfeld, P. Lemkau, & B. Justice (Eds.), *Public mental health: Perspectives and prospects*. Beverly Hills, Calif.: Sage Publications, p. 185.

Smith, J. M. B. (1975). Abstract, *Social work consultation: Implications for social work education*. Doctoral dissertation, University of Utah–Salt Lake City.

Consultation for Consultants

To extend consultation services and make most effective use of existing consultation personnel, experienced consultants will increasingly have the responsibility of assisting other, less experienced consultants to increase their skills—through supervision, consultation, and in-service training. As a result, the present pool of experienced consultants will spend less of their time in direct consultation and more in efforts to improve and extend the activities of less experienced consultants.

Seasoned consultants should also give increasing attention to unsolved problems in practice and theory, delegating known procedures and techniques to those coming into the field more recently.

My experience at the health department in Texas following my consultation with public health nurses (Chapter 5) will serve to illustrate some of the opportunities, problems, and challenges of consultant-centered consultation, or consultation to the consultant–consultee.

The first phase of the consultation with the health department was relatively "pure." State financial grants for personnel were not involved, so the consultant–consultee system relationships were not "contaminated" in this respect. Consultation with the public health nursing staff was primarily client–consultee and administrative–supervisor–consultee centered, with secondary attention to program. The group consultation service from the state department was discontinued after several years as was planned.

The second phase of my consultation was less "pure" in that it was concerned with extending the mental health components of the department through development of a community care services project for the mentally ill.

Efforts were directed toward employing a full- or part-time consultant to the local organization, to be available both to the nursing staff, for more intensive consultation and in-service training, and to the total health department program and personnel. The health department administrator and the nursing director asked me to assist in the development of such a plan.

Research and epidemiological studies carried on by the Division of Mental Health regarding incidence and prevalance of mental illness, mental health maintenance, and experience in development of preventive services substantiated the appropriateness of the Division's entry into this type of activity.

The city health department's interests were compatible with those of the Division's. Although public health nursing service for the mentally ill and their families was not an entirely new service, development of a formalized service-research project was. A written agreement spelled out the interests and investments of both the state and local departments, with both parties agreeing to specific responsibilities in order to initiate and maintain the program. This meant that consultation from the state department, through me, involved some administrative features related to "protection of the investment" (salaries for the local mental health consultant and two public health nurses).

The third phase of my relationship with the local department, operative for several years, carried dual responsibilities. The first was consultation to the local consultant to help him in his consulting and coordinating responsibilities with the nursing staff and community agencies, and in developing other components of the health department program. The second responsibility was mental health program consultation to the health department administrator and nursing director carried out cooperatively with the local consultant.

This complex and varied consultation–administrative role presented special opportunities, challenges, and problems for all concerned. There were few guides or manuals offering specific assistance with this kind of working relationship. The following is presented to identify some of the major issues and to stimulate thought and discussion by consultants, consultees, administrators, teachers, and students in similar circumstances:

1. *Maintaining role clarity and as much freedom as possible* within the consultant-consultee relationship, and recognizing the presence of some monetary and program contaminants. This problem eased somewhat as we learned to acknowledge these "impurities" and understand that there were "authority" implications beyond the more easily accepted "authority of ideas." This insight also helped us identify those parts of the service that were free to be developed in accordance with the local consultant's professional background, interests, system in which he operated, and so on. The freedom in this respect was considerable.

The major boundaries in relation to the Division of Mental Health's investment in the program were as follows: the community care program was to be patient and family focused, with special emphasis on preventive and interventive services provided by public health nurses in collaboration with a variety of community services; the local consultant's role was primarily a consulting and coordinating one—he did not carry out a "social service" program within the health department, although in some circumstances he did provide some direct and referral services.

Eventually the local consultant and I were able to stop and say, at various points in the problem solving: this is now consultation; or this is fulfilling administrative requirements of both systems; or this is an ill-defined mixture of training–consultation–administration–supervision.

2. *Maintaining proper balance and role* in relation to both the local consultant and other significant persons in the consultee system, especially the nursing director and health department administrator, in order to provide coordinated consultation with the local consultant as well as certain services as a representative of an outside organization investing funds in the system.

3. *Assisting the consultant* (through consultation) *to maintain a coordinate role and peer relationship* with directors of services in the department when he had none of the traditional "props" such as budgets, staff (other than his secretary), and the like. Like directors of services, he did have access to the department administrator and was responsible to him, but he did not have traditional administrative authorities and responsibilities. Also, using professional persuasion, he had to see that the mental health components of the program were developed and protected and that services were provided by staff who were not administratively responsible to him.

4. *Personal styles.* Even with the most rigorous controls, my preferences about consultation methods did enter into the consultation relationship. The local consultant's own experiences and work preferences differed from mine. He also had to contend with a substantial history of consultation from the outside (by me), and the problems of transition to consultation from within the organization.

5. *Effects of Affiliation.* The advantages and disadvantages are many in the consultant's being attached to an organization for which he or she has consulting responsibility. Positive aspects are proximity, availability, knowledge of the system, program loyalties, and identifications. On the other side, problems of role clarity, administrative relationships and acceptance, status, and other factors may limit the value of attachments to the consultee system.

In this example arguments on both sides were numerous. The service as carried out was effective and accomplished with a minimum of organizational and operational stress. The arguments for use of an outside consultant, even if one were available, were not sufficiently strong in this situation to recommend a change. Generally in the development of new services, however, both methods for providing consultation should be considered and the decision based on advantages and disadvantages particular to the specific organization, community, and climate.

Epilogue

With the close of this book, the author is reminded of Ezra Cornell's words on the occasion of the opening of his famous university: "There is not a single thing finished." This aptly describes most everything written about consultation. Still more an art than a polished practice it remains a challenge for continuing change and perfection for those who provide, use, teach, or write about it.

Intended primarily as a practical guide, this book may encourage some to probe more deeply into the history and theory of consultation and its contributions to mental health and other human services. For them I would recommend a few books I have found to be particularly useful, already referenced at several points in the text: those by Caplan, *Theory and practice of mental health consultation*, Basic Books (1970); Gallessich, *The profession and practice of consultation*, Jossey-Bass (1982); Mannino, Trickett, Shore, Kidder, and Levin (Eds.), *Handbook of mental health consultation*, National Institute of Mental Health (1986). In addition, these two books were helpful: Ketterer, *Consultation and education in mental health: Problems and prospects*, Sage Publications (1981); and Kadushin, *Consultation in social work*, Columbia University Press (1977).

In continued pursuit of this complex topic, readers may have the thought so well expressed by Cowper in "Winter Walk at Noon": "Knowledge is proud that he has learned so much. Wisdom is humble, that he knows no more."

Appendices

Appendix A provides supplementary and complementary hands-on material to that in Chapter 5, "Group Mental Health Consultation with Public Health Nurses."

Appendix B, appraising formal evaluation procedures and analysis, documents the process and outcome of a three-year consultation experience presented in Chapter 5, "Group Mental Health Consultation with Public Health Nurses." Evaluation of consultation operations, particularly over prolonged periods of time, is sparsely covered in the literature and Appendix B aims at filling the gap.

Data summarized in Appendix B were gathered through a focused interview with 26 participants in the project by an independent mental health nurse consultant from another geographic region.

Appendix C appends Chapter 9, "Education for Consultation—Refining and Enlarging the Effort."

Historically, case recordings of direct clinical services and of supervision have been of great value in the teaching and practice of social work. The recorded consultation conferences and conference summaries in Appendix A, it is hoped, will be a generic contribution to students, teachers, and practitioners in varied human services by conveying something of what a social worker consultant "says and does" in response to some consultee problems in a public health setting.

Appendix C provides prospecti of courses in two Schools of Social Work which include substantial content on consultation theory and practice. Chapter 9 points up the need for refining and enlarging the effort in consultation education and these courses, although not presented as models, represent current and important offerings in which consultation is combined with other practice content. Chapter 9 and other parts of the text have presented arguments for teaching consultation practice, both independently and in concert with related practices such as supervision and administration, at strategic points in graduate education.

Group Mental Health Consultation with Public Health Nurses
Conferences with Supervisors and Nursing Director

Prior to the employment of a mental health coordinator as a member of the city health department staff, I participated in 21 group consultation conferences with the supervisors and nursing director. Topics discussed and their frequency can be grouped under the following headings:

1. Supervisor–staff nurse relationships   14
2. Mental health implications—general evaluation of staff work performance and evaluation of conferencing methods   4
3. Follow-up discussion of mental health conferences (consultant and staff) and appraisal of these conferences   3
4. Child health conference activity   3
5. Meaning and use of authority in supervisory and administrative relationships   2
6. Intrastaff relationships   2
7. General administrative problems   2

Since sometimes more than one major topic was discussed in a given session, the frequency of discussion items (30) is greater than the number of sessions. Topics 4 and 5 above will be dealt with in this Appendix.

CHILD HEALTH CONFERENCES (3 SESSIONS)

The concept of child health conferences, an important and established part of public health service, was well accepted by this health department and its nursing program as a means of providing preventive interventions for infants or young children and their parents who are unable to afford private pediatric services. Consultation concerning the mental health components of child health conferences was requested because the nursing director and her supervisors wanted to improve the program and make it more acceptable and available to eligible children and parents than it had been in the past.

Summary and process recorded presentations on this topic are included here because it came up as a frequent problem in the consultant's conferences with the staff, particularly with supervisors and the nursing director. It was also an activity that the consultant was able to observe directly, both in the initial orientation and on several occasions thereafter on their request. In addition, we all viewed the child health conference as an important avenue for case finding and preventive work by the health department.

Session 1

The first conference on this topic was motivated by supervisory and administrative concern over the small number of families served by the child health conferences, by the need for reorganization of conference procedures, by the desire to reach more families who needed child health conference services, and by concern about the effectiveness of nurse–patient and doctor–patient interviews in the conference.

The consultant's role was to assist with consideration of (1) the human relationship factors in the conferences, (2) the overall emotional atmosphere, (3) interviewing procedures, and (4) parents' and children's reactions to conference procedures. Prior to this session, the supervisors had asked the consultant to observe at the child health conferences.

Following several observations and subsequent discussion with the supervisors and nursing administrator, the consultant gave his summary impressions, which are given below as they were recorded at the meeting. Some of the material was actually presented at different times throughout this conference, not all in one block as it appears here:

> From my limited observation in the child health conferences and in discussions with you, it occurs to me there may be several reasons which prevent parents from coming to the child health conferences. One of the things that impressed me, in a somewhat negative way, is the amount of waiting time these people experience. They are at the child health conference from three to four hours. There are transportation problems; arrangements may have to be made for

other children at home and probably all sorts of other problems facing these mothers. Maybe they have to bring three or four children with them to sit around for hours. Out of the total time they are here, it appears that three-fourths of the time is spent in waiting. Perhaps this is one reason why people do not come back.

Are you saving staff time with this procedure? Are you serving people best when they wait this long? Would it be possible to have a better appointment system? Would it be possible to set up block appointments? Would it be possible to work out a system where parents and children are seen almost immediately upon arrival? Babies are weighed and measured; the baby is examined; the doctor and nurse have their conference with the parent, and then they go home. Would this take more overall time or not? Just from a mental health point of view, this would seem to be a better way of serving the families.

I know you have an interest in improving the mental health aspects of the child health conference service. To do a good mental health job, it is necessary to look at some of the overall administrative operations and procedures in the conferences. The long waiting period apparently frustrates parents, children, *and* nurses. When people have waited so long, can they really use the conference time well with the nurse, after the doctor's examination and conference, or do they just want to go home?

One alternative, as you know, if appointments—block or individual—are not workable, is to make more effective use of the waiting time such as you have done already on some occasions. You know the value of films, group discussions, play facilities, and equipment for the children. If nurses do not have the time for such activities, perhaps volunteer help could be used to entertain the children while the nurses discuss some parent–child relationship topics with mothers.

I do not want to leave the impression that I am sour on the child health conferences. I think it is an excellent service and one which in many ways is superior to what they might get through private facilities. I think too that the possibility for further and more effective service to more people is tremendous.

It has been a stimulating experience for me to observe in the child health conferences, and I appreciate the invitation to sit in on some additional conferences in the future. If I can be of any help after this additional observation, I hope we may have an opportunity to discuss this topic again.

Session 2

The second conference with the consultant on this topic occurred about a year later. During the interval the consultant had several informal discussions on child health conferences with some of the supervisors and the nursing director. He also had an opportunity to observe some other child health conferences in the city. During this time, too, the supervisors, the nursing director, and the total staff had taken a look at the whole child health procedure and were considering certain changes.

Those present were: *

- Mrs. Watson, Nursing Director
- Miss Duncan, Supervisor
- Miss Frank, Supervisor
- Miss Swift, Supervisor
- Mrs. Poston, Public Health Nursing Instructor
- Miss Reading, Medical Social Worker
- Consultant

Mrs. Poston was a former supervisor on the nursing staff. At the time of these conferences she was employed as a PHN instructor at a local nursing school. By mutual agreement of all concerned, she participated because of professional interest in enhancing her mental health skills in nursing, because of contributions she could make to the conferences, and as a way of strengthening relationships between the city health department and the nursing school.

Miss Reading was employed by the city to work primarily with tuberculosis patients, an important public health concern at the time this consultation was carried out.† She, like Mrs. Poston, participated to further her own development, to increase her understanding of public health nursing services, and to improve working relationships between the medical social work and nursing programs.

Session 2 started out in a rather rambling way on several matters of concern about supervision. The nursing director was discussion leader for this conference. Her remarks convey her impatience about projects started but not carried through to her satisfaction. One of these was child health conferences, although this did not come into focus until sometime after the conference got underway.

As with all process recorded material in this Appendix, readers should look "above, below, and between the lines" for nuances and subtleties of meaning and feeling, with such questions as, "What goes on here, and why?" Consider what is

---

*Names are fictitious, and confidentiality is protected by deletion of certain personal material. All participants in these and other conferences were aware that data from this project would be published later in some form. Participants reviewed and critically discussed most of the information in Chapter 5 and this Appendix with the consultant before it was prepared for publication.

†Tuberculosis is *again* emerging as a significant public health problem in certain geographic areas and certain population groups. Representative Henry Waxman (D-CA) decried neglect on TB in *The Nation's Health,* American Public Health Association, April 1990, noting years of underfunding, with the caveat ". . . if more money isn't pumped into the budget, the treatable disease will continue to thrive in children, homeless persons, nursing home residents, and HIV-infected foreigners and minorities."

The prominence of tuberculosis in this book should not be a distraction for the reader. Nursing and consultation strategies concerning the mental health components of work with tuberculosis patients can be applied to other groups of vulnerable clients, such as those suffering with substance abuse, venereal disease, and AIDS.

apparent, or not apparent, about how the consultant does or should simultaneously (1) learn (gather data), (2) feel, (3) observe, and (4) give (see Chapter 1).

In this session, Mrs. Watson said we had been using the previous two meetings to talk about supervision in terms of program planning, budget, improvement of staff, and supervision of staff. She then reviewed the preceding meeting. *She asked if the group wanted to discuss the projects we had started and not carried through.*

MISS DUNCAN: Maybe we don't take time to make plans or think out what we plan. We get off on something else.

MISS SWIFT: We are revising our manual. It is slow but we are still working on it. We started out having a staff conference the second Friday in the month and we are carrying that through.

MRS. WATSON: Each supervisor is responsible for certain programs. We do the same thing year after year and use it for making reports. I wonder why it has been purely report making.

MISS SWIFT: You mean reports and not putting it into use? We don't follow through on the reports?

MRS. WATSON: Reports should be a useful tool in evaluating a program. Does the supervisor have any responsibility in evaluating programs?

MISS SWIFT: It is the supervisor's responsibility when the reports are compiled—we go over them but sometimes we can't do anything about them.

MRS. POSTON: I think I would have difficulty in initiating a new program on the basis of records without having something to do—maybe a time study or the allocation of funds, etcetera. I don't think the supervisor could initiate a new program herself. She would have to have some help. I would need to know how to go about making use of the figures that are in the report.

MRS. WATSON: When you find something that needs to be done, what is your next step?

MRS. POSTON: I think you would need to do a good study.

MISS READING: Reports are on the work that is being done in the group. The supervisors could say, "These changes could be made to improve this particular program." Is that what you mean?

MRS. WATSON: What do reports mean to them and what is their responsibility?

MRS. POSTON: The supervisor could take this up with the staff and point out where they are falling down on a particular thing, like child health conferences.

MRS. WATSON: Does the staff plan the program?

MRS. POSTON: It should be a joint thing. I think the staff should help. You have to determine priority.

CONSULTANT: Would it help to pull out an example and look at it? A history of what happened or didn't happen, like discussing a relationship with the patient. I find it a little difficult to look at it without an example. From what you have said, I gather there are several points you can agree on apparently that need to be done. In reports certain things come out that needed to be done, but later reports show some things still undone.

MRS. WATSON: We have one program we are doing real well. The one I am concerned about is the maternal child health program. Our pre-school program has been down steadily. Last year the number of APs decreased. Our VD program has gone way down. What happened? Are we having fewer mothers with positive STSs? Why are we not seeing preschool children? Why are we making fewer visits to APs? What happened to the child health conference program? We don't have a new child health conference. Why are these things happening?

CONSULTANT: Child health conference is one of the discussions you involved me in some time ago. As I recall there was agreement that the structure of the organization of child health conference should be looked at, and there seemed to be a tentative agreement that in one new conference you might want to experiment a little. In a conference I observed I was concerned about the long waits for the mothers. We talked about serving people more quickly. I was personally curious why this did not come up for discussion again. I assumed you did something that was satisfactory.

MISS SWIFT: The ones that have a long wait come because they want to come early!

CONSULTANT: Even some of those people who don't come before their appointment time wait a long time to see the doctor.

MISS SWIFT: When we put the third nurse down there we thought they would be able to conference the mothers and observe the children. I don't know whether it has helped or not.

CONSULTANT: What else has happened since we talked about it last year?

MISS FRANK: You observed the conference before we had the appointment system. We have saved a lot of the nurses' time.

MISS SWIFT: I think it saves the mothers' time, too.

CONSULTANT: I believe we talked about appointment by the hour also.

MISS SWIFT: We still have drop-ins.

MRS. POSTON: Did this appointment system limit the people you see? If you did not have the appointment system, you would have more people come in, which would increase the number.

MISS FRANK: Some of the parents are assuming more responsibility. They call in and cancel appointments.

MISS READING: Who refers the patient? How do you pick up children?

MRS. WATSON: We don't know how many children are keeping appointments or how many we are reaching.

MISS FRANK: Should we have a report on such conferences as to how many are keeping appointments?

MISS READING: How do you reach the children who are not APs you know about, or people who are recent in the community?

MISS SWIFT: That is where case finding comes in. The nurses have close contact with the families in the neighborhood and they tell them when new people move in.

MRS. WATSON: We can only do it on a referral basis—neighbors, families, etcetera.

MISS DUNCAN: Sometimes something comes up in junior staff conference about something which should be done to let people know about our services.

[There was quite a discussion here about not getting many referrals from Rosedale and Peace Hospitals.]

MRS. WATSON: Unless we get the program better organized, I am not interested in any more referrals, but I think it is something we should look at.

MRS. POSTON: I would like to ask a question. If a student made two visits to a mother and talked about immunization and the mother didn't do anything about it, I told the student not to talk about immunization anymore. Am I justified in telling the students that is what should be done? Do the patients get tired of hearing us talk about immunization and well-child conference?

MISS FRANK: Does this happen to mothers with their first infant?

MRS. POSTON: No, it happens lots of times, and with mothers with several children.

[There was some discussion about why mothers didn't bring their children in for immunization.]

CONSULTANT: What is the largest age group you serve?

MRS. WATSON: Right now it's infants up to a year old.

MISS FRANK: At one time we put all the emphasis on infants, and preschoolers were not stressed. The nurses were told to close them out.

MISS READING: You said you were not interested in any new referrals until the program had been improved. What do you mean? Do you mean in terms of patients, kinds of cases they are getting, what?

MRS. WATSON: We are supposed to be doing a family service. We all agree it's important to give service to the mother before she has her baby and after she has the baby 'till it is of school age. One of our major tasks is to help families be healthy and do it on a family basis. Our whole maternal–child health program is a lackadaisical sort of thing. Last year more babies were born in this city then ever before, but our AP case load dropped. We see practically no preschool children, and yet it is important that we do. We are not giving good family service when we don't carry preschool children. What has happened?

MRS. POSTON: I think you are doing much more with preschoolers than your records show, because we have not been putting anything down on the preschool children. I think your staff is doing more than they are getting credit for.

MISS SWIFT: When we don't see preschoolers in the clinic, we lose a lot of them.

MRS. WATSON: Who makes this kind of decision?

MISS FRANK: I don't let them close out any preschool children.

MISS SWIFT: They aren't doing it now.

MISS FRANK: There is an increase in preschool children's attendance in child health conference. We should do some concentrated work on where these infant deaths occur. Out of thirteen deaths, eleven were not carried. We had more on the north side than in any other area.

MRS. POSTON: Crestwood addition would be a good place for a new well-child conference.

CONSULTANT: What percentage is eligible from the population?

MRS. WATSON: I figured it up in terms of a recent study, and we were reaching about 7 percent who might be eligible. I am not just concerned with getting more people, but I want to do something with the people we already have. We cannot hope to give service to everyone who needs it, but I am convinced that the service we are giving is not what we are capable of giving. I'd like to know why.

MRS. POSTON: How does the staff feel about how they are doing?

MRS. WATSON: How do the supervisors feel about it?

MISS SWIFT: It seems we make a lot of visits to the maternity patients. On the records this morning, half were maternal, infant, and preschool. The staff will visit TB patients and let everything else go. They feel they have to do this.

MRS. WATSON: What happens if they don't visit TB patients?

MISS SWIFT: Everyone calls and wants to know why they have not made the visit.

MRS. WATSON: They make the visits because somebody checks on them?

CONSULTANT: What happens when they break several child health conference appointments?

MISS SWIFT: The nurses visit and see why.

CONSULTANT: Have you ever tried to put together a list of all the reasons why they don't keep their child health conference appointments?

MRS. WATSON: No one ever says to a nurse who is not seeing an AP or an infant in a certain length of time, "Why haven't you seen them?"

MISS SWIFT: We have no way of checking these unless we pull all the records. I think we are top-heavy with TB patients. *[See footnote, page 122.]*

MRS. WATSON: It has priority because it is a well-supervised program.

MISS SWIFT: Another reason our TB program is so good is that we have a chest clinic. If we had the OB clinic, we could follow them up and do a much better job. We have nothing to do with the OB clinic at all.

MISS FRANK: What do you do in AP clinic?

MISS SWIFT: Get names, addresses, blood pressure, bloods, etcetera. I think it does have something to do with nursing services. When you refer a TB patient, you know they are going to be seen; when you refer an AP, you don't know what is going to happen.

MISS READING: Is there any possibility that you could work out a plan where the AP patient automatically sees the public health nurse first before they see the doctor, or not?

MISS SWIFT: Any patients that are seen, we get the record. The ones that are turned away are the ones we lose. They have no organization in the clinic.

MRS. WATSON: I don't think the AP clinic has too much to do without a program.

MISS DUNCAN: I don't know who comes back. I would like to have a system where you could go through and check and remind the nurses they have not made a visit without checking the entire record.

MRS. POSTON: Could you say, "If you have not seen all of your APs, will you report the names to me so arrangements can be made"?

MISS SWIFT: So many of the APs work and you are not able to find these people.

MRS. WATSON: I think there are ways these things could be done, but I have yet to be asked to help.

MISS SWIFT: I am ready for some help. Maybe when the nurses turn in their dailies, if they had a sheet with their name, the kind of cases, and date of future visit, we could follow up this way.

MRS. POSTON: That is why I think you should make a study of one area and see what happens.

MRS. WATSON: There are all kinds of tools that can be used. Every nurse has a workbook. Every day she turns in her itinerary. She gets calls on the book. There are supervisory tools that can be used. Are we using them for mechanical reasons, or are we using them for evaluation purposes? Are you afraid to come to me for this kind of help? [This last question was not answered.]

MISS READING: Can we pick up on Mrs. Poston's suggestion about working on one census tract?

MISS FRANK: How about making a time study? How does the nurse use her time?

MRS. POSTON: If you did your census tract study, you might find where your difficulty lies. You would know if staff education was adequate to take care of the needs.

MISS READING: If you were going to make a study of one census tract, how would you do it?

CONSULTANT: What kind of study specifically are you interested in?

MISS SWIFT: We did a time study in Atlanta compiling the amount of time we spent on every service.

CONSULTANT: I am wondering if there are some things you need to consider before you select any area for study.

MRS. POSTON: Do you have some ideas?

CONSULTANT: As a layman only.

One, I am not sure how much you are concerned about this. I see concern around fragments of the program. I don't get some overall kind of concern.

Two, it might be helpful for you as a group, or a committee of this group—a committee made up of one or two persons from the group and one or two from the staff—to try to restate your child health conference program objectives. You might look at what objectives have been stated and how satisfied you are now with them. If they are not satisfactory, try to reformulate from existing knowledge, and new knowledge, what kind of program objectives would be desirable. In your statement of program objectives, ask yourselves who it is you want to reach in terms of ages and groups.

Three, who is now being reached in terms of numbers? Figure the potential number you might reach if you wanted to and had the staff to do it. How many children are you now reaching (infants through preschool)? What census tracts are you serving? Where are the critical areas in terms of high death rates? How many more people could you reach with your existing staff?

Four, sources of referrals. Where do the infants come from? Who sends them? How do you pick them up? Compare three and four in terms of areas, etcetera.

Five, what happens to families who are getting child health conference service? How many drop out? When do they drop out, at what point, and why do they drop out? You might take a certain block of patients and look at the records you have now. You might look at the children in [Bus] Stop 6: Why did they drop out? Why did they break appointments?

After or during this preliminary study, what kind of help, if any, do you as a staff need beyond the help you can give one another in relation to child health conference? If you feel there are certain areas in which you need some help, you could request help, as you know, from the State Health Department, Nursing Division consultants.

During all the discussion, I have been wondering where I fit in. If I fit in, it would be in relation to human factors in child health conference, the overall structure of child health conference as it relates to the meeting of human needs. What does it mean to people to wait? What does it mean to people to have appointments by day or by hours? How does this best serve their needs? What does the existing structure allow in the way of privacy in conferencing? What might be desired? What does the existing machinery allow in the way of time for conferencing with the nurse and the doctor?

In addition, mental health should certainly be a matter of concern, focused on helping children grow up socially and emotionally healthy as well as physically healthy. How does this tie in with time of appointments, conferencing, etcetera?

If you are interested in taking a relook at the program, a committee could then share their findings with this group and the staff. I would think too that you would want to share this with the health department director and the doctors who are now serving in child health conferences.

If we are enough concerned about anything, we usually do something about it. This is so big, I don't think any one person can do it all alone. You have to pool your concerns, your skills, and your efforts.

MRS. WATSON: I am thinking of the question Lucy asked, "Where would you go for help?"

MRS. POSTON: I always come to you.

MRS. WATSON: Suppose you were concerned with a problem and thought something should be done about it in terms of reports to your faculty—who would you go to?

MRS. POSTON: That would depend—maybe the Dean, maybe the Curriculum Committee, or maybe the agenda.

MRS. WATSON: I feel I am not being used enough by the supervisors, and there are many things that are not being shared with me. I have been a little concerned, and I have been asking myself—why?

Madeline Marney, Recorder

Session 3

The third session on the topic of child health conferences was held during the next visit of the consultant, approximately six weeks after session 2. During this interval there had been considerable work on the part of the administrator, supervisors, and the total staff in reviewing child health conference activities. Also teams of observers from the nursing staff had been visiting other child health conferences. Following these observations, they had written up their impressions and submitted them for staff consideration.

A recording of that portion of the session devoted to child health conferences follows:

Those present were:

- Mrs. Watson, Nursing Director
- Miss Duncan, Supervisor
- Miss Frank, Supervisor

- Miss Swift, Supervisor
- Miss Reading, Medical Social Worker
- Consultant
- (Mrs. Poston, Nursing Instructor, was not present)

Miss Swift was discussion leader. She opened the session by saying it was to be centered around child health conference, as we had some new material and the discussion was not completed last month. A general staff conference on CHC showed a lack of supervision.

MRS. WATSON: Several things came out in the staff conference. One was the number of times the nurses came upstairs and downstairs, and there seemed to be no concern about this at all. Only one nurse was concerned about conferencing with the mothers and seeing that the preschoolers were being watched. There was no concern, apparently, over the lost motion in terms of mothers sitting for long periods. There was no concern about the way the conferences are running! Everyone seemed to be very satisfied.

MISS DUNCAN: There has been a lot of discussion in my group about running up and down after records. Some of them would like to have the records back downstairs again. There seems to be more discussion about records than anything else when they talk among themselves.

MISS SWIFT: Could it be an excuse?

MRS. WATSON: It seems that I am the only one concerned about it. It seems to be an administrative concern only.

MISS SWIFT: The nurses are concerned; there are a number of families that several of the nurses have been trying to get in but they just won't come in.

MRS. WATSON: With the confusion down there, do you think the mothers will keep coming back? When it comes to coming up with any good plan about relieving this confusion, nobody has done anything about it. I have been giving some suggestions, but it hasn't helped.

MISS SWIFT: The nurses will have to take a more positive attitude.

MISS READING: Would it help any if each nurse took her case load and wrote a reason why that particular family has not come into the clinic?

MISS SWIFT: When the mother doesn't keep her appointments, the nurse makes a notation on the record.

MISS FRANK: Mrs. Dooley made the statement, "All these mothers give a reason but it may be an excuse and not a reason."

CONSULTANT: Fill me in a little on the background of these reports. What prompted the observations? What were you looking for when you were making the observations? Did you have any special points, or were you just observing generally?

MISS FRANK: We wanted to know just what was happening down there.

MRS. WATSON: How the nurses were using their time.

MISS SWIFT: When we decided to have our staff conference on this, we had to start somewhere. We decided to have these observations made.

CONSULTANT;   Each observer was looking for how the nurse uses her time?

MISS SWIFT: I was interested in what happened to the mothers and the children and how she used the time she was down there.

CONSULTANT: There is so much to look for. I think you need three people to observe in each conference—one to look at the use of time, the mechanics, the flow and procedure; the second to observe the nurses and the doctor; and the third, which would interest me most, to devote herself to the mothers and the children. It might be better to concentrate on two, three, or four mothers and follow them through. Observe what they are doing, their reactions, their expressions.

Follow a mother into the conference with the doctor and observe what kind of questions she asks and what she *doesn't* ask. If she asks about a behavior problem, how does the doctor respond? Follow with the nursing interview after the conference and see what they talk about.

When I observed down there, there was so much to look for. I confused myself because I really did not know *what* to look for. I get the impression that what concern there is, is more about mechanics, schedules, and records rather than about the *mothers* and *children*.

Another thing which seems lacking to me, and there seems to be some consensus on this, is the need for some well-spelled-out objectives in the child health conference. I think it is hard to evaluate what you are doing without looking again at what you are trying to accomplish in the CHC. State these very simply.

You may be trying to accomplish too much. How can you narrow it down? What can you accomplish here in the CHC? What can be accomplished later on? I think if you asked everyone on the staff what they were trying to accomplish in CHC, you would have thirty different answers! You might ask the staff to write down "what do we want to accomplish in the CHC?" You might take all these answers and see if some definite plans could be made for improving the conference.

MISS FRANK: We attempted to develop an outline for child health conference in the manual.

MISS DUNCAN: It might be interesting to find out from all the nurses and get their opinions on "why do we have a CHC?" Do they feel the importance of it?

MRS. WATSON: A good deal of this goes back to the fact that practically all of the staff came to us with no background in public health. Part of the trouble seems that we did a poor job of orientation into the CHC program. I feel there has been a lack of involvement on the part of the staff and the supervisors in this program.

MISS SWIFT: Would it be possible for some of our nurses to visit the clinics in place and see what they are doing?

MRS. WATSON: I would have to know whether the nurses are interested, and whether they have good conferences in place. What's wrong with the communication? We have talked about this for so long, but nothing has been done about it.

MISS SWIFT: Maybe we don't understand what you want us to do. Since we have some more nurses in the clinic, I don't think it runs as smoothly. Maybe we should have the same nurses for each week; it might cut down on some of the confusion.

MISS READING: What would you think about just putting a staff nurse in to observe and not put any supervisors in?

CONSULTANT: It would be interesting too if you could have the nurses who are working there write down *their* impressions of this conference. What did I like about what happened? What didn't I like? How was I using myself? What mothers would I have liked to talk with more? Why didn't I; why couldn't I? What did I like about what the doctor did? What did I not like?

MISS FRANK: Why do we have to have twenty-four children?

MRS. WATSON: We felt the doctor could see twelve children in each conference without too much trouble.

CONSULTANT: I notice in several of the reports there seemed to be a lot of concern about eating in the morning (sandwiches and candy bars). One of my most vivid impressions was this group of mothers and children in the waiting room looking very bored and unhappy. They sat there resignedly. I didn't see much social activity. They didn't look to me like they were happy about this experience. There was no organized effort to involve the children in play, or much to make the mothers feel more comfortable.

MISS DUNCAN: Another thing, instead of the mother just bringing a baby or her own children, she will come in with a group of adults with that one child and they will all wait and wait.

MISS FRANK: What is the setup in the new building?

MRS. WATSON: Good physical facilities.

[Mrs. Watson and Miss Frank both told about child health conferences they had observed in Pennsylvania and California.]

CONSULTANT: I think this is where a relook at your objectives would help. You seem to have a good staff, and I think they are as enthusiastic as any staff. Perhaps they may be in a little bit of a rut. This is something that is done; it is the way it has always been done. They are so involved in the doing that they may fail to stop and ask, "Why are we doing it?"

MISS DUNCAN: There seems to be a weakness that the nurses are overlooking, and that is behavior problems. I think the nurses are taking a negative attitude toward them.

MISS READING: How much chance do the nurses have to talk to the doctor before the conference?

MRS. WATSON: They can do that if they wish; Doctor Moore is always available.

CONSULTANT: I think if it is possible it might be well to devote a short time for the nurses and the doctor to have a conference about what happened in the conference.

MRS. WATSON: I never have a feeling that the nurses really know the mothers who come to the conference. I have yet to go down there and see a nurse talking to a mother unless she is conferencing her. I never see the nurse just talking to the mothers just to be talking to them. If they have any time to spend talking to anybody, they spend it talking to each other.

MISS SWIFT: I think that might be true, but they have to remember if they talk to the mother, they have to talk to all the mothers or some damage might be done.

MRS. WATSON: This is a freezing place down there—it's cold and absolutely no warmth down there at all. I don't think the mothers are going to become offended if a nurse talks to one and doesn't talk to each one.

MISS SWIFT: I don't agree. I think if you talk to one, you should make it a point to say something to all of them. Some mothers are shy and if you don't talk to them they feel they are not welcome. I think the nurses could spend the time they talk among themselves to talking to the mothers making them feel welcome.

MRS. WATSON: Doctor Moore gives wonderful instructions; she tells the mothers everything they should know or want to know.

MISS SWIFT: I think the nurses could eliminate some of the post-conferences, as the doctor gives them such good advice I think the nurses could spend that time in just being friendly to the mothers and asking if they have other things to talk about.

CONSULTANT: I think the post-conference with the nurse could be useful. It was my impression that this time was not as productive, and the nurses did not give the mother an opportunity to say what was bothering *her*. She did not give the mother an opportunity to say she knew what the doctor said and did not need additional instructions from the nurse.

MISS DUNCAN: Why did that mother come to CHC? Did she come because the nurse told her to? What was her reason for coming?

CONSULTANT: This could be one of the most useful parts of the whole conference, if you can create the *atmosphere* that they are free to talk about anything that they want to talk about. The conference up to this point has been rather formal, but now they can talk about anything they want to. The overall impression I have is a rather formal, mechanical process.

Find out first from the mother whether repetition is necessary; she may not need to have the nurse go over the instructions. She may want to talk to you about something entirely different. If they have to wait, the waiting will have to be more interesting. I don't think the two nurses who are working the conference will have time to do the work and involve the mothers. Maybe an additional nurse should be there to talk to the mothers, show a little film, work with the children. There are lots of films which would be of great benefit to the mothers.

MISS SWIFT: Maybe we haven't gotten over to our families how important it is to talk to our nurses before or after the conference—maybe they don't feel free enough. As far as the waiting, the longest time was two hours and this patient came in one and one-half hours before her appointment was due.

MRS. WATSON: We have spent another morning talking about CHC. What have we come up with?

MISS READING: I think some good suggestions and ideas have been presented this morning.

CONSULTANT: I think the new conference you have set up would be a wonderful opportunity to try out some of these ideas. This is an opportunity for a fresh start and taking a new look. How might you make this one be different?

MISS SWIFT: I feel like the nurses at the south-side conference will be able to pick up some new mothers in the area and the conference will be successful.

MRS. WATSON: All I know is we are not getting the population we should be serving. Last year the amount of money we got was doubled and we didn't use it, so this year we probably will have our money cut back.

CONSULTANT: I do think you have taken some important steps in relooking at your CHC. I am convinced the potentialities are here; you have an excellent staff; the enthusiasm is there if it is captured. However, before anyone can be enthusiastic about anything, she has to know why she is doing it. I don't know whether your staff feels this is an important part of public health nursing or is something they do because it has been done for years and years. I think you are going to have to give them some guides and some framework to take a new look. The place to start is where they are now. You have to know what their present concept is of child health conferences. . . .

Madeline Marney, Recorder

Child Health Conferences: Summary and Questions

The three sessions with the consultant were conducted over a period of fourteen months. There was activity about conference revisions following each of the sessions with the consultant, some of it known to him, some not. There was concentrated activity following the second session, including planned observations. These were not as thorough or as human-relations focused as the consultant thought would have been desirable.

They subsequently worked to improve these observations and implement appropriate actions. These were reported informally to the consultant in conferences with staff at all levels, but there were no more formal sessions with him on this topic.

Questions for the Reader

1. What evidence, or lack of it, was there of progress made in rethinking child health conference philosophy and strategies as a result of each of the conferences and all three of them?
2. What were the primary supervisory concerns?
3. What were the primary director concerns?
4. What was the primary role or roles of the consultant in:
   conference 1?
   conference 2?
   conference 3?
   overall?
5. How might he have proceeded differently in each or all of the conferences? Why?
6. What advantages/disadvantages were there in having nonstaff people in the conferences:
   nursing instructor?
   medical social worker?
7. How might the presence of nonstaff people complement, detract from, or make the consultant's role easier or more complex (in this and similar consultation circumstances)?

MEANING AND USE OF AUTHORITY IN ADMINISTRATIVE RELATIONSHIPS (2 SESSIONS)

This is one of the later topics supervisors and nursing director discussed with the consultant. Although the subject had come up indirectly in many of the earlier sessions, this was the first time it was singled out as a special topic for discussion in an entire session.

Exactly what may have motivated it at this particular time is not known to the consultant, but from the recording that follows it is fairly obvious that supervisor–staff nurse relationships, supervisor–director relationships, and inter-agency relationships had been a matter of concern for some time.

Session 1

In the first session the discussion was almost entirely theoretical. Sometimes it came close to practical application, but apparently there was not sufficient comfort or readiness as yet to take it beyond a stimulating, although somewhat painful intellectual exercise. Note the consultant's several unsuccessful attempts to promote greater depth and real-life application in the discussion.

Session 1 on authority was useful, however, as a necessary prelude to the second session on the topic, which included a lot of down-to-earth work on everyday authority problems, both with nurses they supervised and with the nursing director. (See Consultant's Summary, page 143.)

Those present were:

- Mrs. Watson, Nursing Director
- Miss Duncan, Supervisor
- Miss Frank, Supervisor
- Miss Swift, Supervisor
- Mrs. Poston, Nursing Instructor
- Miss Reading, Medical Social Worker
- Consultant

Miss Duncan was leader of the group today, and she opened up the meeting by reading an excerpt from a magazine article, "Jumping with Authority" (source unknown).

> There's really very little reason to compare authority to women, except that comparing things to women is always interesting. The more you have of either, the greater the temptation, and that is about as far as the comparison can go.
>
> Whatever authority you have over others in your work is given to you for a purpose, not just because you're a good fellow or because somebody thinks your ego needs a little boost!
>
> A large organization cannot be entirely democratic; certain individuals must have authority to say "yes" or "no" or "get this done tomorrow," or "wait until next week before you try that."
>
> Until electronic brains or trained armies of orangutans can take over all of people's work, there is no substitute for authority in varying amounts.
>
> Authority, however, without its partners, cooperation and enthusiasm, is a dull instrument. A little time to explain, a few words of appreciation, an expression of confidence, help to cultivate these partners. It is easy to use

authority to make somebody "jump at the word go." It is much harder to create the desire to "jump."

Give the other person credit for intelligence—share the reason why something is important to you, to the organization, and to that person. Help develop initiative in others by telling why and saying thanks. The rewards will be shared by all.

Miss Frank made the comment, "Even a mosquito doesn't get a slap on the back until it starts working."

Miss Duncan explained that in the supervisors' conference they talk about staff problems and how they handle them. Miss Swift added—"And how we handle *ourselves!*"

Miss Frank asked if we had any problems.

MRS. WATSON: I am real interested in supervision in relation to authority, in terms of your feelings about supervision.

MISS DUNCAN: One of the difficult things is when we feel something has to be done, how do we get it across to the other people to make them want to do it?

MISS SWIFT: It goes back to what authority has meant to us, even in our home situation. I think a great deal of how we supervise depends on how we were supervised at home.

MISS FRANK: What type of supervision we had in our past experiences.

MRS. WATSON: Do you think your supervision is an authoritative thing?

MISS SWIFT: I think more of supervision being guidance and helping individuals bring out their best points. But a certain amount of authority has to go along with it.

MISS DUNCAN: What is authority?

MISS FRANK: It depends upon the position you hold. It can't be entirely democratic; sometimes you have to be direct. It depends on the situation.

MISS DUNCAN: What is the supervisor's place?

MISS READING: Supervision does have some authority back of it. You have to have the authority and policies of agencies back of it.

CONSULTANT: What do we mean by authority? I gather we are thinking of authority, but much of what you are saying means "authoritative"; that authority is a negative thing.

MISS DUNCAN: A very authoritative thing can be a very autocratic thing.

CONSULTANT: Is this authority?

MISS DUNCAN: It could be, but it should not be.

MISS SWIFT: Authority is the right to make certain decisions. It may be to demand certain performances. Authority is the right to do certain things.

CONSULTANT: What do we think of when we are thinking about people in positions of authority? What kind of people are they, and what do they do?

MISS DUNCAN: Authority could be dictatorial or democratic. In a group process it is democratic; when one person is doing it, it is dictatorial or autocratic.

MRS. POSTON: I was thinking in terms of teaching. I was comparing it to persons in positions of authority. The person in authority should make the final decision as to what has been arrived at. This could be in groups or with another individual.

MISS SWIFT: A person who has authority has obtained that position by their capability, and to me I feel I should follow their decisions as far as possible.

MISS READING: There are lots of people in authority who are not there by actual ability, having gotten there by other means.

MISS DUNCAN: What I meant was, how do we get the group together to make them want to work together?

CONSULTANT: Are supervisors authorities?

MISS FRANK: She is just another member of the health team. She has been given additional responsibility to help her staff solve problems through closer work.

MRS. POSTON: I think she is. I think the supervisor does have authority.

MISS DUNCAN: What is needed to make an organization run smoothly?

MISS SWIFT: Understanding of human behavior.

MISS FRANK: She must understand basic needs of supervision, but they must fit the basic needs of the individual.

MISS DUNCAN: To satisfy the need of the supervisor and staff both.

CONSULTANT: What does authority have to do with running an organization smoothly?

MISS SWIFT: I think it has a lot to do with it; the way the individuals in the organization feel about authority. The supervisors are responsible.

CONSULTANT: Do you need authority?

MISS SWIFT: I feel we need authority in everything.

MISS DUNCAN: Can we change the word *authority* to *relationship?* It can be authoritative or direct leadership.

MISS SWIFT: There may be two or three different types of authority: one, like the army, or two, authority where it is a more democratic thing, where individuals do have some say in making decisions.

CONSULTANT: Is authority consistent with democracy?

MISS DUNCAN: In some respects, yes.

MISS FRANK: It could mean that you are well informed in your particular field.

MISS DUNCAN: Where acute decisions do not have to be made, "yes," but for other decisions, "no."

MRS. WATSON: Do you think it is inconsistent?

CONSULTANT: Authority and democracy are two separate things? In a good democratic society we don't need authority? *[Raised as questions]*

MISS SWIFT: Yes, we do.

CONSULTANT: Aren't we thinking of authority in a negative way? We are thinking it is a necessary thing, but a nasty thing. We need it for protection, or for emergency matters. Are you authorities in this organization?

MISS SWIFT: We need authority in everything. We have the privilege of making decisions.

MISS DUNCAN: We are working with individuals. We are working with the community. We are trying to help.

CONSULTANT: What does this have to do with authority? Apparently there is some concern about authority, so let's look at it. If it is too difficult or unpleasant, let's say so and we can look at something else.

MISS READING: Authority can be one type or another. It can be positive or very negative. It depends on the person who is in the position of leadership or directorship.

MRS. POSTON: Does it apply to evaluation?

MISS READING: Do you think of authority as a person who knows his subject and whom you can go to for help?

MRS. POSTON: That is the way I look at it. I assume that by position one becomes an authority.

MISS DUNCAN: Does position give authority?

MRS. POSTON: It implies growth and improvement. I don't think position gives authority.

MISS FRANK: I like to think of authority as one who knows her field and to whom I can go for guidance. I don't want to think, "Well, she's boss." That throws a different light on her.

MISS DUNCAN: Authority could mean a helpful, not a dictatorial person.

MISS SWIFT: Not someone that cracks the whip.

MISS READING: There are different ways of cracking the whip.

MISS DUNCAN: There is a difference in authority that is group delegated and authority that is delegated by one individual.

CONSULTANT: Do you think we need authority?

MISS READING: How could we function without it?

CONSULTANT: I don't know, *I* need it. To me authority means someone who has earned her or his way to be in a position of leadership—administrative, supervisory, consultants in all kinds of situations, in business, health, welfare, education. But there are some people who have not earned their way who are in positions of authority.

MISS READING: Could you respect a person who is in a position of authority who has not earned it?

MISS SWIFT: It would depend on who it was.

MRS. WATSON: It depends upon where you stand. You might have a dictatorial attitude coming from a different direction.

CONSULTANT: What responsibility goes with authority? Can we say he or she has earned the right to be in authority? The right to do what? How should this authority be used? Authority at different levels. To me you are all in positions of authority but at different levels.

MISS DUNCAN: Doesn't that bring in how to work with people? Arrive at decisions? To listen?

CONSULTANT: That is pretty big. Don't you think of yourselves as authorities? If you don't think you are authorities, don't let my "authority" make you think you are! I am quite certain the staff nurses look to *you* supervisors as authorities, and supervisors look at Mrs. Watson as an authority.

MISS DUNCAN: Don't we look on the staff as an authority?

CONSULTANT: Their patients do.

MISS READING: We all get a certain amount of satisfaction in being looked at as an authority.

MISS FRANK: You can make the staff too dependent on authority.

MISS DUNCAN: Or they can become that way themselves with too much authority.

MISS READING: Is it good authority if you make your staff too dependent?

MISS SWIFT: It can work in the same way when the staff can make their families too dependent on them.

CONSULTANT: I don't mind you looking on me as a minor authority. I feel I have something to contribute here in helping you integrate mental health into public health nursing practice. But I don't do it for you, or tell you very much. What responsibility goes with my authority?

MISS SWIFT: You motivate us.

CONSULTANT: If I have earned my way to do this, how do I do it?

MISS DUNCAN: How we help ourselves to help others. The things we do, the things we say in helping others.

MISS SWIFT: I have to bring in getting the job done. The right person for the right job.

MISS FRANK: Improvement of the services in nursing along the lines of mental health would be your chief good. You want us to show some improvement.

MISS READING: I think the supervisor should know what she is doing.

MISS SWIFT: Along with authority we should correct and commend.

CONSULTANT: If you can accept that you are authorities, how do you feel about being an authority? How did it happen you brought this subject up this morning?

MRS. WATSON: I have a feeling that the group feels that authority and supervision are synonymous.

MRS. POSTON: They are.

MISS DUNCAN: The thing is to make a democratic thing out of it instead of an autocratic thing.

MRS. WATSON: You are saying supervision and authority are synonymous and they are not good.

[The group said they did not think this was so.]

MISS SWIFT: I don't think it's bad.

MISS FRANK: We think it's good when we satisfy the needs of the staff and they can cope with their daily routine.

MISS DUNCAN: If we feel there is a need, how can we make the other person see the need?

MISS SWIFT: Before an individual is able to help anyone, they have to experience getting help themselves so they can know how to help that individual. Maybe through our supervision they have not gotten that help. How can they give it until they themselves have gotten it?

CONSULTANT: You could say to a nurse about some case, "I don't care what you think, you are to continue working with the family." Or you can agree with her, but you may feel your administrator may have other ideas so you can say, "Well, nurse, we have to stay in there."

MRS. WATSON: I think we are skirting away from authoritativeness. Supervision is a helping role with an administrative responsibility. What does the administrative responsibility entail? The helping role that is done in terms of the job. Working with staff and families seems to be an educational thing where authority may or may not, as you see it, be of the same type. The authority then involves professional skills and techniques, but authority in terms of administrative responsibility is something else. It seems to me that this is what this group is skirting. This is the part of supervision this group is rejecting. We cannot accept administrative authority because it is something that we don't like very much.

MISS SWIFT: I feel like I accept it.

MRS. POSTON: It has to do with growth.

MRS. WATSON: I am thinking in terms of ourselves—how do we feel about administrative responsibility that connotes authority? . . . I gave an illustration of what she meant and than asking [sic] the group how they felt about telling their staff, "You can't do this."

MISS DUNCAN: It doesn't bother me.

MISS SWIFT: There are some things we hate to tell the staff nurses.

MRS. POSTON: I think sometimes we don't think through the whole process. I think it goes back to earning the right and sharing it with the group even though it may be something you don't like.

MISS SWIFT: If it is a group decision, you don't mind telling the staff, but sometimes there are other things you don't like to tell the staff.

MRS. WATSON: There are a lot of policies that I don't like. We accept them and do it, or accept them and don't do it.

MISS READING: You hate to do things where you have to say, "You have to do this, or you have to do that." Some of us don't like the responsibility of saying "no."

MRS. WATSON: A good supervisor also has to be able to set limits. Some of these limits have to do with personalities and individualities.

CONSULTANT: Where are we?

MRS. POSTON: It looks like Mrs. Watson wanted us to say sometimes her job isn't always pleasant, but sometimes our job isn't either.

MRS. WATSON: I didn't mean that. I like being a supervisor and I like being an administrator. I know I am not always a good supervisor or a good administrator, but I hope that I can learn as I go along how to be a better one. There are certain things I have to do that I don't like doing, but I hope I can do them well if I have to do them. I sometimes have to make decisions that nobody likes, even though they know why I have to make them, but I am going to keep on doing the best job I can in being a good administrator in terms of authority, a good administrator in terms of professional skill, and in helping everybody I can to reach maximum satisfaction in terms of their own performance and give to the community the help they want.

MISS FRANK: I think you can tell whether we like our work. It is reflected in our work.

MISS SWIFT: I like being a supervisor. I don't know whether I like it because I satisfy my own needs, or because I want to see some of my nurses meet their needs.

CONSULTANT: I think you all like being supervisors, but I am not sure you like being "authorities"—or facing the fact that you are authorities. If it is true you don't like being authorities, it is because the connotation of authority is bad. It doesn't need to be at all. It is necessary; it is useful; it is important.

MISS DUNCAN: Sometimes where you have to make decisions and the staff balks, it is unpleasant. It isn't as much now as it used to be.

CONSULTANT: You think about how the staff nurses look on you as an authoritative person; you are a little uncomfortable in this role. You accept the helping, guiding, and evaluating role of supervisor which is part of authority but there are some nasty things about authority you don't like. If we could have gotten at these nastier things earlier, that might have been more important to look at this morning.
[*Pause*]

CONSULTANT: It might help sometimes to look at administrative responsibilities which are part of the supervisory pattern which trouble you and try to understand them. Think about making them less troublesome and less difficult to accept. There is a difference between supervision and consultation. You are entirely free to accept or reject anything I may bring. I have no administrative responsibility for you. If you were not good supervisors, a mental health consultant could not function . . . .

Madeline Marney, Recorder

Questions for the Reader

1. Why do you think the topic was chosen for discussion?
2. What is your evaluation of this session?
3. What was your impression of the discussion leader's contributions?
4. What were the consultant's contributions?
5. How might he have handled the discussion more effectively?

Session 2: Consultant's Summary

At the conclusion of the first session on authority, even though it ended somewhat "up in the air," no plan of continuing the discussion was mentioned. However, when the consultant met with the group a month later, they stated (no advance alert) that they wished to continue the discussion. They also agreed that some of the primary issues had been evaded in the first session. The earlier part of the discussion that followed, like the first one, consisted of some further theoretical explorations of authority, including a dictionary definition of it.

Gradually, however, they brought the discussion around to consideration of authority implications in their supervisory relationships with several staff nurses in particular, and later to their own relationships with the nursing administrator. Finally they considered some problems in the overall administrative structure which made it difficult to use authority in a creative, positive way in supervision and in numerous day-to-day nursing activities.

The consultant's primary role in this session was to help them look at what they themselves had said they were skirting. Also, through their expression of feelings about negative connotations of authority, he helped them to look more comfortably at their own rules as "authorities" and in their own use of the supervision they received from the nursing director.

Conferences with Staff Nurses

There were numerous conferences with the consultant on work with patients, and all of the group sessions were recorded either mechanically or by a secretary in some form. The most frequently used method was shorthand. Summaries were made available to all participants after each session in preparation for the next session, and for selected publication use later.

Although valuable for the reader, to present an example here of a process recorded account of consultation on work with patients is difficult. The reasons are several: size of the group (average 15); and meaningful presentation and analysis of the interchange without conveying relevant information about the individual participants and their responses (confidentiality).

For these reasons, therefore, the first staff conference reported here is one with a staff nurse *committee* to help plan a workshop. The group was smaller, and the content is less personal than one about interactions with patients. I believe, however, that even with these limitations the process recording will be of value as a supplement to the text on consultation strategies.

This particular conference was selected for inclusion also because it illustrates informal evaluation of what had taken place earlier in consultation and the value of previous sessions regarding both content and method. It is an illustration of frequent "soundings" the consultant initiated at strategic points throughout his work with the staff to test "how we are doing" so as to make needed corrections to improve the interchange between consultees and the consultant.

The committee had asked to meet with the consultant to get his help in planning a workshop on *Group Process*. The consultant took the liberty of first discussing some related concerns about group reactions to the consultation conferences as background for workshop planning.

EVALUATION, GROUP PROCESS, AND WORKSHOP PLANNING

Those present were:

- Staff nurses Mrs. G., Miss K., Mrs. F., Mrs. W., Mrs. T., Miss P.*
- Mrs. Watson, Nursing Director
- Miss Frank, Supervisor
- Consultant

Consultant said he understood that some in the two staff mental health consultation groups were a little tired of case conferences.

CONSULTANT: This is something you didn't bring out directly in the group conferences, but it seems important for us to look at together in this meeting of the committee. You have also expressed interest in group process and group dynamics.

In our discussions up to this time we have been more interested in the case material than in looking at *ourselves* and how *we* are functioning individually and collectively in the group (group process). Perhaps we might use this meeting as a practice session in looking a little more closely at how we work. Mrs. F. has agreed to serve as observer. She will be taking some notes and will be reporting from time to time on her observations of our group behavior.

I also understand you want to do some planning for the future and have discussed plans for another workshop. Before we talk about that, however, could we take a quick look at the past?

I would like for you to discuss, as freely as you can, some of your observations about how we have been working together in our group sessions. I think it is healthy that you can say that you are tired of case conferences. I should like to have you say, if you will, *why* they are boring and why they have not been meeting your needs. Without this it is a little difficult to plan for the future.

[There was a long pause in the discussion here.]

MRS. G.: I feel each conference has been a help to me in one way or another. I think when we are bored and say we are not getting anywhere, the fault is that we have not been putting enough into it. The subjects are broad. I feel that I could do better than I do. We are the ones

---

*Initials and names are fictitious.

who will benefit, and if we don't apply ourselves, we will not get much out of it. As long as we have been having these sessions we should grow and get deeper into them.

CONSULTANT: If we took a look at ourselves now, we might ask why we were all silent at first and why we seemed to breathe a sigh of relief when Mrs. G. broke the silence just now.

MRS. T.: Maybe we were all groping for words. I certainly was not bored, but maybe I was dissatisfied. I got the feeling when we were choosing a case that I was just looking through my case load and seeing if I couldn't use this one. I don't want to give up case conferences, but I think we need something new.

MISS P.: When we pick out a case study, we select our *worst* one and present a case that has a lot of problems. We should select one with less problems; then perhaps we could do something with the major problems instead of trying so hard on all of them. *[See Chapter 5.]*

MRS. W.: We have had something of a repetition in our cases. I really feel that way, but I enjoyed all the case conferences. Sometimes when I go into a home I am at a loss as to just what to do. I feel I have a lot to learn.

MRS. G.: I still like role playing—I think it helps more than anything.

MRS. W.: I have always been shy of role playing.

CONSULTANT: You mean you think we should have done more role playing and worked harder at it?

MRS. G.: Yes.

MISS K.: Role playing does play a very important part. I think it makes the case more realistic and more observable.

MRS. F.: I was wondering if all of us had not been a little frustrated. We present a case, and the first thing you know there are a lot of little problems we did not know were there. When they are brought out, it makes us feel very uncomfortable!

MISS P.: It makes you feel maybe I am not as good as I ought to be.

MISS FRANK: Does it in your home visits?

MISS P.: Yes, after they are pointed out to you.

CONSULTANT: This is an important point. We could all meet together and talk about "cozy" things. One of us could make a speech. That would be very comfortable, and maybe even helpful. But I think any real learning, particularly in human relations—nurse–patient relationships—if it is to be effective, does involve some pain. We don't set out to make these sessions painful. I think you know I don't deliberately try to make them painful or to make you uncomfortable. But in the process of learning and taking a closer look at ourselves it is sometimes painful. Should we try to avoid this?

MRS. T.: I don't think we can learn very much without some pain.

CONSULTANT: Is it *worth* the pain—is it worth the effort? Is this also a part of your dissatisfaction with the conferences? We don't need to go on with these conferences indefinitely, as you know. After several years of working together, at least with some of you, do our discussions make your job more difficult? Easier? Are you where you were, a little further back, or where do you think you are?

MRS. W.:   I think the conferences have helped me quite a bit, even the cases I presented. I feel more comfortable in situations than I did before I started. I can talk to families better. I can look at things the way I think the *families* look at them and feel about them.

CONSULTANT: If you do feel you have made some progress in your job, remember the mental health conferences have been only one small part of your progress. You are older, more experienced; you have had more supervision, more contacts with families. You know your co-workers better.

MRS. G.:   When you start out you are real sympathetic, but as your load gets larger and larger—if you don't have something to make you feel for your patients, you would really get hard-boiled. *burn out!*

MRS. T.:   The fact that we would like to do something about our child health conferences, the fact that we know that we are not giving the patients everything they need, show that we have gotten something from these discussions. I can now tell when I am not giving these people the things they need.

CONSULTANT: One of the things I am curious to know is your impression of what is "mental" in public health nursing. How do you see it? What does mental health in public health nursing mean to you?

MRS. T.:   When I first came on the staff I felt that public health was more of a mechanical thing. I didn't think of the effect you would have on people, and the effect they would have on you. Mental health is in all of our dealings with people—as public health is—it is not something you can set apart.

MRS. F.:   When we first starting discussing mental health, on the way to a visit I would be riding along and be thinking of the "mental health" I would *try* on them. But now I don't. Now I think mental health is not just something that needs mending, but a total part of my job.

MRS. G.:   Mental health goes deep into feelings of individuals and helps you see them and create a better understanding. It makes you more patient with the individual.

CONSULTANT: I would agree. Mental health and public health are inseparable. I am glad you could share some of these thoughts and feelings with me. If we couldn't talk about them, I would be seriously concerned about our work together!

[At this point the consultant asked Mrs. F. if she would like to make some comments as an observer. Note above she had been an active participant in the discussion.]

MRS. F.:   It has been just an hour. I was wishing we had kept a sociogram. The first twenty-five minutes everything was directed at the consultant. Nothing was directed to the group. The group was relaxed. Interest level went up. All of the group were verbal, but no one took all of the conversation.

CONSULTANT: During the first twenty-five minutes all the action was directed toward me. Why did it change? How did it become a more shared process? Why were there peaks, and why were there lags? If we were to take a deliberate look at group process, we would carefully consider these changes and the reasons for them. . . .

At this point the group indicated that, because of time limits, we needed to work more specifically on plans for the workshop. They brought out two primary concerns for workshop attention:

1. *Interviewing,* specifically in the setting of the child health conference. Miss P.'s statement was illustrative of this concern: "We visit the mother as an AP. She has a baby, we visit her, and she will not bring the baby to clinic—why not? That is our problem. We go back when the baby is eight weeks old, and she still has not been in. We ask her why, and the excuse is very thin. Maybe our interviewing is not good. Maybe we did not get across how important it is to bring the baby in to child conference."

2. *Group Process.* This interest was sparked particularly by the fact that two of the staff nurses had recently attended a workshop elsewhere on "group dynamics." Their interest was contagious and also fitted in very well with the current needs of both discussion groups at this stage in the consultation process. These two nurses were also very much interested in trying out some of the theoretical ideas that had been presented in the workshop, as applied to their work in the mental health consultation sessions.

Post-Conference Planning (Workshop)

During the summer the local planning committees continued to meet on their own to develop plans for the workshop. In addition to content and procedure they discussed leaders for the workshop. They concluded that they would like to have the consultant serve as workshop coordinator and to have his colleague, the mental health nurse consultant from the Division of Mental Health, assist the consultant and also serve as a resource person. After the mental health nurse consultant had joined the Division staff, she had accompanied the consultant on one of his visits to the local health department and observed several of the group sessions with the consultant, as part of her orientation to consultation and in-service training activities of the Division. She was known to a number of the nursing staff also through her participation in statewide workshops which they had attended.

After further local planning, the committees met with the consultant for refinement of the workshop plans and objectives. It was agreed that the workshop would have a twofold focus: interviewing and group process.

The discussion of *interviewing* techniques and methods would be supplemented with case materials. The specific objectives with regard to interviewing were:

1. To sharpen interviewing skills
2. To develop better awareness of self in professional activities
3. To develop better awareness of the patient and her or his total needs
4. To develop increased understanding of mental health concepts and their application as an integral part of public health nursing

The deliberate look at *group process,* it was hoped, could be achieved, not through use of group process as a separate workshop topic, but through the discussion of interviewing. By this means there would be deliberate and continued efforts to look at how the group was functioning. The specific objectives related to the focus on group process were:

1. To develop better awareness of total group functioning
2. To develop better awareness of the individual functioning in the group
3. To assist in helping the group assume more responsibility for its own direction as to how problems are to be discussed, continued evaluations of group performance, leadership, etc.
4. To assist in making this a practical exercise for more effective functioning in all professional group activities

In addition to the general planning committee, several subcommittees were appointed: to select case materials and films, to develop a bibliography on interviewing and group process, and to arrange for workshop housing, transportation, and refreshments.

WORK WITH VD PATIENTS

From time to time, the consultant attempted to record some of his own impressions of certain conferences but was not very faithful in this respect. Because of heavy personal investments in the conferences, making meaningful summaries of them, or indeed even making selections from them, was a formidable task.

The following example, therefore, is simply an attempt to illustrate conference method and point out some of the major areas of discussion in one conference. This conference occurred shortly after regularly scheduled consultation services with staff nurses began.

Following the presentation of case material, the consultant assumed a fairly active role in helping the group focus on:

1. What were some of the most important problems
   as viewed by nurses
   as viewed by patients
2. The nurses' *feelings* about patients and their problems
3. Desirable goals in work with them
   immediate
   longer range
4. Possible supports, strengths, and obstacles in achievement of goals (patients and nurses)

Summary of Problem

The case problem was presented by Mrs. Ambrose,* following discussion with her supervisor, for the purpose of talking about feelings of embarrassment and discomfort, and what to do about them, in work with VD patients. In an earlier staff planning conference the group had agreed that this was a rather common problem for many of them.

Mrs. Ambrose frankly admitted her concern about this problem, which caused ineffective work with VD patients. From the early discussion after presentation of the case, it appeared that her feelings and concerns were shared by a number of nurses in the group.

The problem concerned a family consisting of a 25-year-old mother with a diagnosis of late syphilis, a 26-year-old father who was employed at a steel mill, and two children, ages two years and six months. Referral to the nursing division was made by the VD clinic. Home visits were planned to encourage treatment at the clinic for the mother and VD examination for the father.

The work with the mother had gone along fairly well, although Mrs. Ambrose at first had some difficulty in establishing contact. Her main concern was with the father, whom she had seen on two occasions at home but who still had not come in to the clinic for examination.

Mrs. Ambrose stated that she had handled her contacts with the father very badly, was embarrassed in talking with him, and did a poor job of interpreting the need for examination. She said she was afraid she would "insult him" on the first visit (at home—interviewing on the porch, wife inside the house). Mrs. Ambrose said she did not know what to say or how to say it, and instead of talking very much with the man, she handed him some literature on VD and left.

---

*Fictitious name.

Group Discussion

There were three general concerns. First the group talked about the kinds of feelings nurses experience in work with VD patients. After listing and talking about a number of these, they attempted to examine why such feelings exist. Included were such things as the delicate nature of working with a married couple when it is known that one member has VD—fear that the nurse's presence around the VD problem may aggravate the marital relationship; the social stigma attached to VD; the sexual connotation of the problem; the opinion that it was generally more difficult and uncomfortable for nurses to work with male VD patients than with females.

Following this they talked about possible approaches in work with this particular family and with VD patients generally. It was concluded that perhaps too much emphasis was placed on VD, in a rather mechanical sort of way, without the nurse's appreciating and understanding more thoroughly the *people* who have the disease—the need for perhaps a "total health approach" in work with such families, keeping in mind that the patient may use other health department services more easily if attention is focused on the total family picture rather than just on VD of one of its members.

The group also talked about the importance of not pushing too fast in attempting to get patients to follow through, that actually progress may be more rapid if early efforts are slower and concerned primarily with building up a good working relationship.

Consultant's Impressions of Discussion

The discussion was of considerable interest to most of the group members. It was not too difficult for them to describe some of their feelings about their discomfort in working with VD patients, but it was hard for them to look at why these feelings existed. Even though the discussion on this point came with strain, there was also a good deal of thoughtfulness once we got a little beyond the superficial.

Some of the same discomfort that they discussed in regard to work with VD patients seemed to be present in this group discussion. It was particularly hard for them to look together at why it was usually more difficult to work with male patients. Although it was not possible to go into the dynamics of this in any very intensive way, they said recognition of the problem at least was helpful.

APPENDIX B

Appraising Outcomes of Mental Health Consultation

Dorine Loso, Mental Health Consultant in Nursing, USPHS Regional Office, Denver, Colorado

What actually happens—what developments take place, what gains occur—in the course of an extended program of consultation afforded to the public health nursing staff of a local health department by a mental health consultant of a state health department?

The Division of Mental Health of the Texas State Health Department undertook to answer this question with a specific group of public health nurses in a city health department after three years of monthly consultation sessions with a psychiatric social worker from the state agency. Should the service be continued? Should it be offered to other local agencies? What had been learned as the result of the experience that could be shared with other mental health consultants and enrich general professional understanding of theory and techniques employed in the consultation process? And how can the outcomes of such intangible, dynamic interpersonal and intragroup interaction really be appraised?

Even these questions appeared too broad, too general, to answer directly.

What goes on in consultation from the viewpoint of the consultee? What changes have been brought about in the consultee? These questions could be answered subjectively, but with some degree of objective insight, by the consumers of the service through interviews conducted by an outside investigator

Revised by Wendell Williams, Mental Health Education Consultant, Division of Mental Health, Texas State Department of Health. Dr. Williams later became Director of Training at the Denton State School (Texas). Before his recent retirement he was associated with the Continuing Education Program, School of Social Work, Virginia Commonwealth University. Following this assignment, Ms. Loso worked for a number of years as Director of the ADAMHA Regional Office in San Francisco.

who was familiar with public health nursing and with the theory and application of consultation in other settings.

The purposes and nature of the appraisal were agreed upon by administrative officials of the two agencies, state and local. The method to be employed was the focused interview, administered to the entire group that had participated in the consultation: the nursing director, five supervisors, and twenty staff public health nurses.

An out-of-state mental health nursing consultant was secured as interviewer through cooperation of the Dallas Regional Office of the U.S. Public Health Service and the National Institute of Mental Health in Washington. Background of the project and purposes of the evaluation were outlined by the Division's Research Consultant, Wallace Mandell, and its Mental Health Nurse Consultant, Charlotte Bambino. Wording of the questions was the responsibility of the interviewer, with refinements suggested by the Research Consultant to increase the effectiveness of data collecting in light of the overall research design. The Consultant Psychiatric Social Worker who had been conducting the mental health consultations deliberately absented himself from these conferences to ensure maximum objectivity of the appraisal.

The nursing personnel were well oriented to the nature and purpose of the appraisal. Conference room space for the interviews was arranged and a schedule set up and adjusted as necessary. The fullest possible cooperation was afforded by the Health Department Director and every member of the staff. Interest and willingness to participate in the study are exemplified by a nurse who was on educational leave but home for vacation, who came for the interview, and by several former staff members who returned to be interviewed despite having small children and other home duties.

All together, 26 persons were questioned about their participation in the reactions to the consultation experience. At least 14 of the 26 had attended as many as 28 sessions of the monthly mental health conferences during the three-year span. During this time they had met in three work groups, two of them including both supervisors and staff nurses, with times arranged, to allow maximum participation within the framework of their regular schedules. The third group was limited to supervisors of public health nurses.

Following the series of 60-minute interviews, responses were tabulated and grouped into natural categories. (See complete list of questions on page 173.) Summarized answers to interview questions provide the basis for later interpretation of the data.

SUMMARY OF INTERVIEW RESPONSES

Responses are grouped to shed light on two major areas of concern: (1) What goes on in consultation from the viewpoint of the consultee? (2) What changes, if any, have been brought about in the consultee?

What Goes On in Consultation
from the Viewpoint of the Consultee?

Eleven questions were judged to have a bearing on the query.

Question 2 From your past experience, what do you think consultation is?
Six responses reflected a perception of consultation as *information exchange or
stimulation of ideas:* "Consultation is a way to develop ideas; . . . to stimulate
thinking and having a positive approach; . . . an exchange of ideas to try to come
up with answers to problems (two responses); . . . a drawing in of additional
information, then talking about situations hoping for a solution; . . . consultation
with others about others' problems and getting opinions to get help."

Eight responses defined consultation as *help from outside persons with
special training:* "Consultation is professional help from a person able to do
it; . . . a person trained in mental health assists in everyday problems; . . . at
your request, someone who has advanced knowledge helps you see the problem.
Doesn't do it for you but gives you assistance; . . . consultation is more than
giving of help—it is asked-for guidance by a person of advanced education."

Seven persons described the consultation process as *group problem solving:*
"Consultation is a tool to cause you to think, to evaluate yourself and the problem
in order that you can solve the problem; . . . find out, talk over with someone
else, discuss problems to do a better job; . . . listen to what others say, and when
and why, and select an answer; . . . group consultation, discuss families and
problems and work as public health nurses with someone who understands;
. . . discussion of subjects by one or more persons to attempt to come to a
working plan; . . . to talk over with others your problems and get others'
opinions for help; . . . a pooling of thoughts, ideas, and facts toward a goal of
solving a problem."

*Question 3 What do you feel has been the goal or purpose of these
meetings?* Responses to this question tended to group themselves under four
types of answers: (1) understanding behavior and attitudes, in others and self; (2)
improving skills in work groups; (3) improving skills in working with families;
(4) accepting different behavior and attitudes.

*Question 5 What kinds of problems do you think of bringing to the mental
health sessions?* brought an interesting tabulation, one that provides data for
significant interpretation in a later section. Problems associated with tuberculosis,
unwed mothers, and child behavior were the most often recurring:

Problems Brought to Mental Health Conferences

Tuberculosis	21
Unwed mothers	13
Child behavior	13
Alcoholism	7
Multi-problem families	7

Problems Brought to Mental Health Conferences (continued)

Tuberculosis and alcoholism	5
Maternity	5
Interviewing	4
Crippled children	4
Venereal disease	4
Adolescence	4
Interpersonal relationships	3
Marital difficulties	3
Geriatrics	3

Question 6 What part did you take in the sessions? Here the answers related to the methodology used at the conferences. Most of the group indicated that they had group roles of observer, leader, and recorder which they had practiced in their group sessions. Most of them had participated in presentation of case histories during mental health conferences. Several indicated they had done process recording. Two of the supervisors stated they participated in the sessions as resource people.

It began to be apparent that the interviewees' responses reflected their feelings about their initial participation in the conferences and these feelings were also reflected in some of the other answers and throughout the material of the entire group. In several responses to question 6, interviewees indicated how uncomfortable they felt initially in the conference: one indicated she felt uncomfortable when there was silence in the sessions; others stated that they did not become active in the beginning because they did not know what was going on or what was expected of them.

Question 8 Have you been more interested in some of the sessions than in others? The responses depended on what was being discussed, when, and why. What was discussed seemed to be a major factor. One significant, and fairly frequent, response was that after the group knew what the sessions were going to be about and when they felt they knew what was going on, they were most interested. Some of the other responses indicated more interest when they presented their own cases, less interest when they had other work pressures, boredom with seeming repetition or feeling that a session was too long. However, none of these represented any general group judgment.

There was some favorable response to an orientation session during a recent mental health conference. Frequently mentioned in response to the interviewer's opening invitation, "Tell me about one of your mental health group meetings," this orientation session seemingly had been a very successful and satisfying experience for those who participated.

Question 9 What were you looking to get out of these sessions? brought the following categories of response: (1) understanding self and self-improvement, (2) professional development, and (3) learning how to deal with people.

Question 10 Do you see the purposes and goals of the supervisors' group and the staff groups as being the same? A majority of responses were affirmative. Some indicated they hadn't particularly thought about this but felt the goals should be the same; two felt the goals should be different. That participants had not considered this relationship appears significant in connection with the next question.

Question 11 Is there a sharing between staff and supervisors about what is discussed in each group meeting? Some felt there was sharing; an equal number felt there was not; some were not sure. Again, this was the first time that many of them had thought about this particular aspect of the conferences. Some of the supervisors stated that they did share some of their conference ideas with members of their own staffs; some of the staff nurses reported informal sharing between the two staff groups, but on no regular or formalized basis. No interviewee expressed strong feelings as to whether there should be a sharing.

Question 19 If a new nurse on the staff asked you what mental health consultation was, how would you answer? Most of the group indicated they would tell the new nurse not to expect answers to problems. The majority suggested they would try to describe the conference as thought provoking but difficult to understand how to participate in at the beginning. Some felt the new person would need to experience being in a few sessions before she could understand, and no advance describing would give her this understanding. Some indicated they would attempt to tell the new nurse how the consultant functioned in the group as well as how the group used each other for problem solving. It seems apparent that the group members were stating what they themselves were unprepared for when they approached the sessions, as well as the difficulty of describing to anyone the mental health conference experience.

Question S-4 How would you see further help being utilized? was answered in a variety of ways. For some, the amount of mental health consultation service presently available to the agency seemed sufficient and this question had little meaning. Others suggested the desirability of having a consultant "on the spot" when problems arose rather than saving them until the two days each month when the consultant came. While the majority of the group felt that a full-time consultant would be "ideal," several expressed satisfaction with the present arrangement and suggested that more consultation might make them dependent and less apt to think for themselves.

What Changes Have Been Brought about in the Consultees?

Other questions allow a shift of focus from the nurses' perceptions of the consultation *process* to its *effect* on their thinking and performance. Whether or not consultation had accomplished anything in helping the nurses improve the quality of their work was the second major area of concern which this study sought to illumine.

Question 4 Thinking back over some of these sessions, can you illustrate or give examples of how these purposes or goals (question 3) *were accomplished?* brought the following comments:

> I used to feel the need to tell patients to do this or that. Now I have more patience and think of patients' readiness. I *suggest* now, rather than *tell*."
> "The conferences caused me to stop and think of the patient as an individual."
> "Now I am concerned how patients feel about what they want to do and I have them participate in the planning."

Other comments included: "I realize now that one can't get help just from experience alone! . . . helped me to stop and listen to patients; . . . learned that one couldn't change the world; . . . helped with TB work, especially when people are cool to nurse's visits; . . . learned to listen and not take sides or be critical; . . . acceptance of people's living pattern; . . . help to realize nurse's feelings toward certain patients and their families."

Question 7 Has your participation changed over the course of these sessions? How? elicited a type of "before and after" responses represented by the following:

In the Beginning
1. "No basic information."
2. "Frustration—first held back."
3. "Difficult to know when to ask for help."
4. "Didn't know what was going on. Ill at ease."
5. "Wanted more from consultant."
6. "Didn't know or mean much in beginning."
7. "Expected more from consultant—especially answers."
8. "Felt I needed to participate each session."
9. "Had previous experience."

10. "Constrained in the beginning."
11. "Hesitant to talk—might say wrong thing."

Current Participation

2. "Feeling of sureness now."
3. "Freer to ask."

4. "More at ease."

5. "Do not expect this now."
6. "Now participate at will."

7. "He expects us to do more thinking."
8. "Can go or not go without guilt."
9. "Encourage participation of all."

10. "Freer to talk more."
11. "Freer now to say right thing or not. Say what I want to."

12. "Antagonism because I had to go."

12. "Now see value to sessions, especially when I present case."

13. "Didn't feel confident—didn't know what it was all about."

13. "Understand reasons for sessions."

14. "First just listened—didn't feel free to talk."

14. "Now bolder—will speak up right or wrong."

15. "Always feel easy to talk."

15. "Feel more responsibility to group now (discussion as good as I am good)"

16. "Silence."

16. "Now easier with silences."

17. "Uneasy and easily frustrated."

17. "More confident and sure of self."

18. "Didn't know what was expected of me."

18. "More at ease now—can speak up right or wrong."

19. "Never been afraid to speak up."

19. "Enjoy more now."

20. "Used to formal kind of in-service."

20. "Opinion more important and questions mean more."

21. "Uneasy in the beginning."

21. "Easier to take part in groups."

Question 12 Do you view your supervisor any differently as a result of these sessions? brought a majority of affirmative answers. Five responses indicated no change, and two were neutral. Most of the responses were of the following type: "I see my supervisor as an individual with problems, too; . . . I can speak more freely to my supervisor; . . . I have a better understanding of what her job is; . . . I understand the tasks of supervision more; . . . I feel there is more help now to work together."

Question 13 Does the monthly meeting influence your staff group in working with each other as co-workers? brought three types of response: (1) it was helpful, (2) discovered common situations, and (3) improved relationships or feelings of togetherness.

Responses to three additional questions, all designed to get at consequences of participation in the consultation process, tended to fall into four categories. The questions were: (16) *How do you think you have been helped the most?* (17) *What differences can you see or feel about your work that you can attribute to having the mental health meetings?* (18) *What from the sessions have you been able to apply most directly to your work as a staff nurse?* The consequences that may be summarized from the responses were: (1) sharing problems with work groups, (2) understanding and acceptance of patients, (3) stopping and thinking, and (4) understanding and accepting of self.

Another approach to evaluation of consequences was through questions asked of supervisors.

S-1: In relation to your supervisory conferences with staff, can you see evidences of application both in the staff nurse and in yourself? There was agreement that application had been made. Some felt that staff nurses were better able to focus the kinds of help they wanted from their supervisors; also they were able to ask more meaningful questions and to make better use of the help supervisors were able to give.

S-2: What kinds of influence have you observed in the staff nurses' work? Again there was general agreement that staff nurses had increased their effectiveness. Supervisors felt that staff had a better understanding of families and their problems, and also that the nurses could relate to their families with more self-understanding. In addition, the supervisors felt that the staff had a better understanding of each other and were able to get along better with co-workers as a result of their group meetings.

One of the supervisors felt she could tell improvement in record-keeping and that this related directly to the kind of help her staff nurses were receiving in the conferences. The supervisors also generally felt that they themselves had received a great deal from the conferences as members of the staff group as well as from their own supervisory sessions with the consultant. They viewed these latter sessions as an opportunity to discuss some of their problems with staff and receive help.

One of the supervisors expressed the feeling of more staff unity and closeness between herself and the staff as a result of sharing problems in the conferences. It was general consensus that mental health conferences helped the staff nurses to see that mental health was a part of total health programming and, as such, a part of every home visit.

Summary

Responses to individual questions began to fall into patterns and pieces began to fit together. Perceived goals or purposes of the mental health conferences appear to be (1) understanding behavior and attitudes, of self, patients, and others, (2) improving skills in work with work groups, (3) improving skills in work with families, and (4) accepting different behavior and attitudes.

These purposes relate closely to what individuals hoped to get out of these sessions: (1) understanding self and self-improvement, (2) learning how to deal with people, and (3) professional development.

For this group, goals and anticipated outcomes seem generally to be paralleled by what they actually felt was gained by these mental health conferences: (1) understanding and acceptance of patients, (2) understanding and acceptance of self, (3) sharing problems with the work group, and (4) learning to "stop and think."

INTERPRETATION OF INTERVIEW MATERIALS

Nature and Method of the Consultation Process

An analysis and evaluation of the consultation process as it took place in a city health department with the assistance of a consultant psychiatric social worker from the state department of health produced a step-by-step picture of the development of the consultation process that may have broad applicability.

To trace this development, we will examine the initial expectations of the nurses and why they had them. We will examine their initial reactions to the experience and consider why they continued in spite of the "growing pains." We will look into differences in participation as the conference series progressed, changes in perception of the consultation process, changes in staff ways of functioning, and changes in supervisory or administrative functioning.

From Expectations to Understanding

Expectations influence the participants' perception of an experience as well as their participation in that experience. The expectations of these public health nurses and their supervisors in relation to goals and purposes and expected outcomes of the mental health sessions have already been reported. We now turn to the whole area of expectations related to the *process* of the experience itself.

Despite the orientation provided prior to the monthly group sessions with the consultant, there was almost universal opinion expressed by the staff that they were uncertain as to what to expect in the beginning sessions. They did not feel they knew what was expected of them as members of the group, nor how they should participate (question 7).

If they did not know what was expected of them, they knew what they expected of the consultant: *answers* to problems. He was an expert in mental health; he should not only have the answers but also be able to tell them how to solve their problems. They also wanted the consultant to spell out their role for them, what to do and how to participate in the group. One thing they did not expect of him was a knowledge of public health nursing, for they all agreed that it was important to orient him as to how public health nurses function in this health department (question 14).

Growing Pains

The slow growth of understanding of the consultation process, what the consultant does and what the consultees do, can be traced through a series of steps revealed by the public health nurses' responses to the interview. A similar listing of steps could be found in any analysis of the educational process, but these nurses had their own problems and needs which came out in the process, directed its development, and ultimately validated its consequences.

Step 1. The consultant was expected to provide answers to problems and resolve tensions experienced by the public health nursing group. While requests for assistance were couched in terms of health problems, the deeper underlying problem for the public health nurse seemed to be her difficulty in coping with a difficult balance of roles she is called upon to play in her work.

On the one hand, she is the representative of a public health agency with the obligation and authority to enforce health regulations and safeguard against infractions of these laws. This is clearly outlined, both by her education and experience and by health department policies, local ordinances, and state law. She has—and represents—authority. (See recording of session with Supervisors and Nursing Director, Appendix A.)

On the other hand, she is called upon to play a very different role by the nature of the way in which she works with patients and their families. She comes into the family situation as a friend, seeking to understand the various factors bearing on the presenting health problem and to encourage the family to assume the greatest possible amount of responsibility for handling their own problems. The public health nurse attempts to see the family in their situation, from their viewpoint; she assumes a role in alignment with the family and becomes "theirs," as psychologically close as possible for a professional worker to be.

It is difficult, if not impossible, for her to be viewed as a close and helpful friend and at the same time the representative of an external authority whose commands may conflict with their wishes or readiness to act. This conflict of role is also the source of tension within the nurse who respects the family's feelings and at the same time must follow health department regulations.

This conflict of loyalties is reflected in the responses to question 5: working with TB patients was mentioned the highest number of times by the group. The nurse has specific regulations she is sent to interpret and have the patient agree to; in some instances, this means getting the patient to agree to leave his home for sanitarium care. Since she is aware of the communicable nature of the disease, isn't it harder for her to see the problem as a patient sees it? Could the hostility that many public health nurses experience be a result of their failure to be the health workers they would like to be? Is it hostility to the health department authority which she symbolizes that interferes with her ability to function as a friend of the family?

In looking to the consultant for answers to problems, public health nurses seemed to be seeking also the resolution of tensions and frustrations arising from the dual nature of their role. Thus the presenting problems of dealing with the TB patient appeared almost overshadowed by the frustrations and difficulty of working with this type of patient with satisfaction in the working relationship. This was the unvoiced expectation we have verbalized in the statement of step 1.

Step 2. The consultant refused to accept the request for "answers to problems." Almost universally when the group began to feel that their expectation of receiving answers or being told explicitly how to solve problems was not going to be met in that fashion, they experienced frustration and disappointment with resultant confusion and hostility. These feelings were expressed and discussed openly and frankly by most of the interviewees. Many expressed resentment that the consultant did not give his opinions but tried to have them think through the problems themselves. Some described consultation (questions 1 and 2) in terms of what it was *not* based upon in their initial experience. For example, many said it was not getting answers to questions or it was not being told by someone what to do about a problem.

Their disappointment was evidenced in such statements as, "I didn't know why he didn't tell us what to do," "He just sat back and seemed unconcerned," "I felt he should have the answers," "Would have saved a lot of time if he had just told us."

Step 3. The nurse group continued to stay in consultation conferences despite frustrations. The planning for these conferences had been made initially upon the request of the city health department. When the staff experienced disappointment with the beginning meetings, they did not, however, ask for them to be terminated. One could suggest that despite their disappointment they felt that perhaps in later sessions they would be more satisfied, or perhaps they did not have much freedom in choosing whether or not to remain. It was apparent that the nursing administrator felt that kind of conference very worthwhile for her staff, and her interest and approval may have been a strong factor in the staff's remaining in the conference.

Step 4. Over the hump. The consultation process as the conferences progressed is best illustrated by the responses to question 7, which dealt with change in participation. Slowly the nurses began to feel that they "knew what was going on" and began to feel "easier in the group"; "they could feel comfortable with silences" and were able to "speak more freely."

They were feeling more comfortable also in regard to the consultant as they began to sense his acceptance of them and their problems. They became more at ease, too, as they became accustomed to small work groups, and they dealt with their initial disappointment by trying to "see what the consultant had in mind." Initially, some felt constrained to speak for fear of "saying the wrong thing," but as the meetings progressed they felt freer to speak up "right or wrong." This change seems to be quite directly related to step 5.

Step 5. The nurses discovered the consultant was accepting their situation. Gradually, then, the expectations of the nurse group began to shift. They perceived that the goals could be realized through a different method than "being told answers." They began to be stimulated to think about the problems presented and to explore their own ways of solving them, as well as to take responsibility for their solution. This is never an easy process; as one nurse described the consultant's quiet insistence on their doing their own thinking, "It was ·like squeezing blood out of a turnip that wasn't there." But they began to find that talking with each other and thinking about their own problems was satisfying.

Step 6. The nurses discovered that other public health nurses have similar problems. The use of the small work group as a vehicle did a great deal to facilitate this step, for by sharing their problems with each other, they found they were encountering many similar situations in their work. The sharing itself encouraged the groups to exchange their thoughts and ideas about the family situations and, encouraged by the consultant, the group sought to use themselves for problem solving.

Step 7. The nurses were more able to accept emotional support from each other. As the group was able to gain help from each other through sharing problems, they were able to move to step 8 and in turn to step 9 and 10.

Step 8. The nurses were more able to accept their work situation, such as "frustrating patients."

Step 9. The nurses joined with each other to use the consultant as a helpful person with certain skills.

Step 10. The nurses and consultant could realize their goal together.

Thus the process had completed its first cycle, from original expectations, through gradual understanding of the process, to the formation of new expectations and new insights into effective ways of participating in the mental health conferences, all on the basis of personal experience. How did this come about?

Dynamics of the Evolution

Four factors may be credited with the change of perception and growth of understanding in the consultation process: (1) relationship with the consultant, (2) group relationships, (3) supervisor–staff relationships, and (4) methodology of the consultation provided.

Relationship with the Consultant. In the beginning, because of the realization that the consultant was not going to assume a teacher–pupil direct-telling role, the nurse group expressed disappointment toward the consultant. The consultant's holding to his belief and not yielding to their demands was an important factor in their eventual shifting of their expectation of him. This beginning period is a crucial one for both consultant and consultee.

As the consultant began to be perceived as being able to listen and be accepting of the problems, even though not assuming the responsibility of solution, the nurses began to relate to him. They began to define how each would function in the group and gradually saw him as a resource person, a thought stimulator, occasionally as one who refocused the group's discussion, and one whose opinion could be sought along with opinions of others in the group. The group accepted now that he "helps us to think and talk about problems," that he "helps keep discussion moving," that he "helps you see where you go from there," and that "he doesn't say much but gives food for thought."

With acceptance of the consultant role, some of the group attributed their initial discontent to their unwillingness to buckle down to think for themselves and to their unfamiliarity with this kind of conference. Their acceptance of the consultant now is apparent in their genuine warmth as they speak of him and their current sessions.

Group Relationships. Another factor influencing the change in goal perception was the discovery in the work groups that the nurses had similar problems. Sharing with each other afforded them an opportunity to gain new ideas about working out problems. The kind of support they were able to give each other extended outside the actual work group setting, as is illustrated by some of the responses to question 13: "It was helpful to talk with one another," "helped to share problems—gave staff a feeling of togetherness," "provided a way of working together to consider one another as individuals in the same way as patients."

Supervisor–Staff Relationships. From the beginning, supervisors participated in the small work groups. One of the supervisors who had some experience in group work was a part of both groups. As the sessions progressed, the staff nurses began to feel differently toward their supervisors (question 12), making such statements as, "I can speak more freely to her," "I can see them as individuals with problems too," "I understand their position better."

Supervisors also felt that these sessions enabled them to know their staff better and to work more closely with them. As mutual understanding increased, supervisors and nurses could be more supportive of each other and facilitate the reshifting of expectations of the work groups.

Methodology of the Consultation. The vehicle of small group consultation was a very real factor in the process of consultation. The groups were small (10 to 15) and were held fairly well as closed groups. One of the groups, which had more change of participants because of nurses leaving the staff and other factors, showed less productivity and more restlessness and dissatisfaction.

To some of the staff, working in small groups was a new experience, and part of their early uncertainty might well have been due to this fact. However, as they began to experience how they might help each other, the group sessions were described more positively by them. In the later sessions they requested more specific help in increasing their skills in group dynamics, and this request was met by the consultant and other members of the state mental health division staff through a workshop and continuing small group sessions. There seemed almost universal agreement that the practice of these work roles in their small groups was very satisfying and helpful to them. A few indicated they felt too much emphasis had been put on this practice and expressed the desire to go back to the original way of participating in the small group, with more active consultant participation.

The size of the group allowed for full participation. Also, a sense of togetherness began to develop and there seemed to be an increased feeling of unity among group members. There was not much indication of sharing between groups; the groups seemed to remain distinct from each other as the sessions progressed.

It appears that the methodology of the small group set the stage for the staff to discover their mutual problems, to explore their common ideas, and to talk over different approaches to problems and experience the satisfaction of group problem solving.

Proof of the Pudding—Change in Staff's Way of Functioning

The ultimate appraisal of any experience can be most effectively gauged by the changes in functioning. Several of the interview questions were used to gain information about this. Illustrations were sought of work situations for which they felt their approach and work were now different. Such questions also helped sharpen and clarify the staff's own feeling of a changed way of working. There were five areas of change, as expressed by the group: (1) in work with patients, (2) in work with each other in small groups, (3) in work with supervisors, (4) in work with other agencies, and (5) in personal gains. "As sauce for the pudding," staff supervisors reported changes in their ways of functioning too.

Work with Patients. In this, and the other areas, there was one recurrent expression indicating change in the nurses' approach to patient problems: as a result of these sessions they now would "stop and think." Because this was specifically mentioned so frequently, it seems to have particular meaning for this group. It might indicate a definite weighing of the presenting problems and more deliberation before they felt compelled to act. It would also indicate that they felt more comfortable thinking through problems with patients rather than having to take immediate action. One nurse stated that before the sessions she felt she went into homes to *tell* people what to do but now she tried first to "really determine what was the problem" and to "see the individual in his way of life" and "not press my will into his" but "encourage him to use his way to solve his problem." Another nurse stated she felt more comfortable working with patients now because she no longer felt the need to know all the answers. Another said she was more understanding of individual patient's feelings now that she stopped to think about the family situation; she also said, "When you do, you are more apt to have a good feeling that you've done all you can."

Many in the group felt they changed their way of working with patients from a telling role to one of seeking to determine with the patient how he might like to handle his own problems. There was a general expression of greater awareness of their own behavior and its effect in their working with patients.

Some saw their changes in attitude resulting in a difference in the nursing care or services offered. For example, several expressed their attitude change about "lazy," "unwed," or "dirty" patients and about cultural and minority groups. Their change in patient care was evidenced by an increased ability to see patients "as individuals rather than TB or OB cases" and to "let people help themselves."

There was an increased attempt to view problems as families saw them and to be conscious of how differently patients and families responded to stress. Also it was evident that the nurse gave added importance to *listening* to their patients before they attempted to suggest any solutions. It was apparent that the conferences increased their sensitivity to the needs and feelings of individual patients and their families. The conferences sharpened their awareness of behavior and its effect on themselves and others with whom they worked.

Work with Each Other in Small Groups. In the group experience the nurses were able to accept support from each other and use each other for problem solving. They also felt a change in their relationship to others in the group, expressed by such comments as "feeling closer," "more able to discuss problems with each other and to profit from their experiences." They felt they learned how to work productively with the other nurses and increased their understanding of individual nurses in the group.

Work with Supervisors. Both staff and supervisors agreed that the mental health conferences had brought them closer together through increased understanding of each other. Both their respective jobs, and the personal thinking and ideas of both groups, were affected.

The staff felt freer to talk with the supervisor about problems as a result of the conference, and they came to feel more comfortable with them on finding out that "supervisors had problems too." The nurses felt the conferences made the supervisors more aware of the kinds of problems the nurses encountered, and they in turn profited from some of the supervisors' experiences with similar problems. Some nurses felt the small group work conferences increased the effectiveness of the supervisor–staff group meetings.

Work with Other Agencies. Sometimes when cases were presented in the mental health conferences, other agency personnel who were working with the family were invited to participate. The nurses felt their presence to be extremely helpful, affording them an opportunity to discuss and plan with staff members of other agencies. It also gave them a chance to learn about how other agency people viewed problems and what services agencies were able to provide. The nurses felt that as a result of such discussions it was easier to work with the other agency personnel about other families when problems arose. Some of the nurses stated they better understood how social workers functioned because of getting to know the consultant.

Personal Gains. Approximately one-third of the staff group mentioned personal gains as one result of the mental health sessions. Four people used this expression to indicate they had received help to understand, accept, or cope with personal concerns in regard to themselves or their families. Three of the group came to feel surer of themselves, especially in a strange or new situation. It seemed apparent, as far as the interviewer could determine, that the nurses had made individual application from the group sessions rather than seeking out the consultant for an individual conference about their personal concerns.

Changes in Supervisor and Administrator Functioning

The supervisory and administrative staff felt they had gained much to improve their way of working with staff as a result of their own sessions with the consultant and as participants in staff groups. Through their own sessions, they increased their ability to work through some problems of supervision. The staff groups enabled them to get to know the staff members better and thus facilitated their working together. They felt more able to handle problems presented by their staff and also felt the conference aided in unifying the nursing department as a whole.

Individually the supervisors felt they were made more aware of their own behavior and more understanding of each nurse's behavior. The supervisors and administrator felt that as a result of the conferences, the staff brought fewer problems because they were better able to cope with them themselves and there was more cooperation within and between the staff nurse groups.

Summary

The consultation *process* as a group experience has been described as it progressed from high hopes and expectations based on some ill-conceived expectations to a productive relationship between staff nurses, their supervisors, and a mental health consultant from the state department of health. Participants discovered within themselves and in each other resources for dealing with their own problems and feelings at the same time that they were gaining insights into working with the problems and feelings of their patients and families.

It may be assumed that the developments reported here might well occur in the same way were mental health consultation introduced to other public health nursing staffs. A number of unanswered questions might be posed and tested in other situations to judge the validity of this assumption.

Would a different type of orientation to the consultation process have been helpful? More effective? Reactions of this group suggest that those who undertake consultation, especially in the mental health area, need to consider very carefully what the staff group may be seeking from the consultant. Perhaps a clearer definition of consultation is an important consideration.

Would this group have experienced more or less disappointment and hostility in the beginning had the mental health consultant been a nurse? It seems particularly evident that this consultant's skill, experience, and willingness to try to understand public health nursing were key factors in his working with this group.

How long should one continue consultation to any given group? When should the local agency assume responsibility for seeking a local consultant to take over the consultant role, and when should this come about?

Participant responses in this project clearly indicate that the group felt these mental health conferences helpful to themselves, in their work with patients, and with their co-workers. As a result of this experience they now have a better understanding of what consultation is and how to use it.

EVALUATION OF THE APPRAISAL PROCESS

Consultation to public health nurses is not new, nor is mental health consultation an untried venture. Many health departments have sought consultation from state departments. However, few have had sustained, consistent consultation by a mental health consultant over a three-year period, nor have their efforts been as carefully documented and evaluated as was attempted in this appraisal.

Instigation of the Appraisal

The mental health consultation was set up at the request of a city health department and provided by a consultant psychiatric social worker from the Division of Mental Health, Texas State Department of Health. Appraisal of the outcomes was initiated after the project was well under way, partly to judge the effect of the service, and partly to determine whether it should be continued, and by whom. Though the benchmark of a preliminary interview was lacking, it was still felt that information from the nursing staff as to their feelings about the consultation process and what effect they felt it had on their work might be useful for deciding whether the consultation should be continued. Remembered reactions, stimulated by the technique of the focused interview, could also throw light on the development of current uses of consultation and changes in staff functioning as reflected in their own perceptions of such changes. Plans for the appraisal were worked out jointly by state and local health department representatives.

Selection of the Interviewer

It was considered desirable that the interviewer be familiar with both public health nursing and mental health consultation. A nurse should readily establish rapport with other nurses and be more objectively critical of a social worker's consultation to nurses. Finally, it was preferable to have someone not from the Southwest and therefore unlikely to be personally involved with this department's nursing personnel and problems.

The interviewer, who was secured through the assistance of the Dallas Regional Office of the U.S. Public Health Service and the National Institute of Mental Health, was a mental health nursing consultant from another USPHS region. There were therefore considerable time limitations for orientation to the project, determination of objectives of the appraisal, and conducting of the interviews. One week was devoted to interviewing, with approximately six 60-minute or longer interviews per day.

Planning the Appraisal

A preliminary proposal was written for the appraisal, and general information was shared about the consultation project with this city health department. Planning sessions included the regional mental health nursing consultant from the Dallas Office of USPHS, the research consultant, and the mental health nurse consultant from the Division of Mental Health. The consultant psychiatric social worker who had been providing the staff consultation deliberately absented himself to ensure maximum objectivity. This group outlined the major areas for the interview focus:

1. What goes on in consultation from the viewpoint of the consultee?
2. What changes have been brought about in the consultee?

Actual development and wording of questions were left to the interviewer, with the assistance of the research consultant. Twenty-four questions were used, 20 with nurses and supervisors, and 4 with supervisors only.

Setting for the Interviews

The nursing staff personnel had been well oriented as to the nature and purpose of the appraisal and seemed well prepared for the interview. Arrangements for conference room space and the scheduling of interviews were ready in advance. Although the first day had been set aside for interviews with nursing supervisors, the schedule was adjusted to allow testing of interview questions with both supervisors and staff nurses. Since interviewees were not expecting dictaphone recording of their conversations, it was abandoned in favor of pencil and paper notes.

Although there had been some staff turnover during the consultation period, at least 14 of the 26 staff members interviewed had attended at least 28 sessions of the mental health conferences. Four nurses no longer with the department came in for interviews, as did one who was in the city during a school vacation. Another former staff nurse was interviewed while at school in the interviewer's home city.

The interviewer was impressed by the willingness and readiness of staff members to participate in the interviews and by the advance orientation and the many other evidences of cooperation on the part of the health department and its staff.

The Focused Interview Technique

The focused interview was selected as the best tool to deal with a complicated problem. The job specifications called for an *ex post facto* appraisal of participant reactions to a mental health consultation service project. The consultation was to be appraised at the end of three years, during which there had been various personnel changes. Mental health consultation is inevitably many faceted and intricately interwoven with problems of nursing and public health administration. Time was limited, both for the interviewer and for the nurses and supervisors.

In planning of the appraisal, it was determined to seek information in two general areas while still allowing the interviewee freedom to give the kind of information she wanted to give. The questions were also devised so as to yield the maximum amount of individual response and minimize sharing of questions between interviewees.

Questions were very much the same throughout, with some refinements of wording at the close of the first day. Order of asking was maintained in all cases unless it meant breaking the interviewee's train of thought as she moved onto a response to some other related question.

While answers to some questions tended to validate others in the total series, related questions were formulated more to get a different slant from the interviewee than to cross-check or validate information per se. The questions were to evoke perceptions, and such questions do not lead themselves to horizontal and vertical totals adding up to the same figure.

The interviewer found little evidence of preplanned responses to known or anticipated questions. Most expressions were each person's individual responses, created out of the moment of question.

More Specifically about Questions

To a reader interested in adapting this appraisal method (and avoiding some of its limitations), some further details about questions and their interpretation may have meaning.

Pretesting and validation of the interview questions would have eased the mind of the conscientious interviewer. For example, does a given question evoke a definitive concept of consultation in the mental health setting or rather in other areas of consultation which she has experienced? Verbatim reporting was followed on this item, but tape or dictaphone recording would have permitted more detailed reporting and analysis of other items where verbatim reporting was impossible.

In looking back, the interviewer felt that several of the questions seemed to yield the best responses and material. These were numbers 2, 5, 7, 9, 17, and 19 (see page 173). Responses to these questions gave a rather clear picture of how interviewees felt about consultation, the mental health group sessions, their participation in these sessions, and what they had gotten out of them.

Question 1 was designed to initiate the interview and gain general ideas about mental health conferences and how they were conducted. Interviewees were free to describe any conference(s) during the session, and there was variety in their selection, depending largely on which conference they felt was most satisfactory to them.

Twin concerns about content developed as the week progressed. The interviewer felt responses seemed too general, not as definitive as the questions might indicate. By the third day, the interviewer began to fear that her familiarity with the pattern of responses emerging might unconsciously color responses of subsequent interviewees. To offset this tendency, the interviewer took down more verbatim materials during the later interviews; future researchers would benefit from either mechanical recording or greater intervals of time between interviews to permit more detailed written recording.

One interesting observation: During the mental health conferences, staff nurses had been divided into two groups to facilitate scheduling. While no effort was made during interviews to ascertain to which group the interviewee belonged, similarity of responses revealed the difference in group experiences represented.

The final question, number 20, which was added after the first day to elicit any additional comments the interviewee cared to make, was found helpful in a few instances. By and large, however, nothing much new was added as a result of this question. This might indicate that the interview had been long enough so that the interviewee felt no need to extend it, or that she felt the questions were sufficiently comprehensive. There were no other signs of fatigue and usually interviewees indicated their willingness to talk even further.

It was generally more difficult to get descriptive material from the supervisors about their own sessions with the consultant. The interviewer wondered if this problem might have been related to the kind of content areas discussed in these sessions. Supervisors' participation in the two staff work groups was seen by both supervisors and staff nurses as helpful and as facilitating closer relationships.

The interviewees were able to express their opinions frankly and openly. Their initial disappointment, confusion, and hostility toward the consultant because their expectations were not being met were, to the interviewer, a free, healthy response, and their being able to talk about it indicated real growth on their part.

From the interview material there emerged definable steps in the consultation process which the nursing group experienced in the course of the mental health sessions with the consultant. These steps, as stated earlier in the report, were experienced by the members of the groups at different times and all indicated the process was a slow, gradual one. As the group members became surer of what their participation was to be, and were able to shift their beginning expectations of the consultant, they expressed more satisfaction in their experience.

One further comment related to generality of nurses' responses: It is difficult to measure quality of a broad answer or the depth and difference of meaning of a term used after several years of additional experience. When some nurses said they had a better understanding of patients' and their own behavior as a result of these sessions, they no doubt meant something different than when they had applied the same term to an evaluation of a workshop held years earlier. The reflection of change in their attitudes and in their work with patients was best gained by specific illustrations. Examination of nursing records as well as observed home visits might have enhanced the evaluation of these changes.

List of Interview Questions
(Used with all nurses and supervisors)
1. Tell me about one of your mental health group meetings.
2. From your past experience, what do you think consultation is?
3. What do you feel has been the goal or purpose of these meetings?
4. Thinking back over some of these sessions, can you illustrate or give examples of how these purposes or goals were accomplished?
5. What kinds of problems do you think of bringing to the mental health sessions? (Now and Past)
6. What part did you take in the session?
7. Has your participation changed over the course of these sessions? How?
8. Have you been more interested in some of the sessions than in others? When, why, and what was being discussed?
9. What were you looking to get out of these sessions?
10. Do you see the purposes and goals of the supervisor's group and the staff groups as being the same?
11. Is there a sharing between the staff and supervisors about what is discussed in each group meeting?
12. Do you view your supervisor any differently as a result of these sessions?

List of Interview Questions (continued)

13. Does the monthly meeting influence your staff group in working with each other as co-workers?
14. In the beginning, in order to understand each other, was it important to learn something of the background of the consultant? Also, was it important to orient the consultant to what a public health nurse does and how the agency functions?
15. Does this kind of interpretation still go on in your meetings? When accomplished, what area is still ongoing?
16. How do you think you have been helped the most?
17. What difference can you see or feel about your work that you can attribute to having the mental health meetings?
18. What from the sessions have you been able to apply most directly to your work as a staff nurse?
19. If a new nurse on the staff asked you what mental consultation was, how would you answer?
20. Is there anything more about the mental health experience you'd like to tell me? (Question added after first day)

(Used with *supervisors only*)

S-1. In relation to your supervisory conferences with staff, can you see evidences of application both in the staff nurse and in yourself?
S-2. What kinds of influence have you observed in the staff nurses' work? (Added to all interviewees after first day)
S-3. Do you think the two days a month of mental health consultation is appropriate and adequate to the needs to the agency?
S-4. How would you see further help being utilized? (Area–method)

Questions Relating to Areas of Focus

- Area I What goes on in consultation from the viewpoint of the consultee?
  Questions: 1, 2, 3, 5, 6, 8, 9, 10, 11, 19, and S-4.
- Area II What changes have been brought about in the consultees?
  Questions: 4, 7, 12, 13, 15, 16, 17, 18, and S-1, S-2.

APPENDIX C

Examples of Graduate Courses—Social Work

The outlines selected from the University of Missouri–Columbia and the St. Louis University are presented as current offerings of substance on consultation, although not necessarily as models.

Selected portions of my earlier writings on consultation were used extensively by these professors. Their encouragement to include them with elaborations and additional materials was helpful in the preparation of this book.

APPENDIX C

Examples of Graduate Courses—Social Work

University of Missouri–Columbia School of Social Work

Supervision/Staff Development/Consultation

Dr. Paul Sundet

COURSE DESCRIPTION

The philosophy, objectives, principles, and methods of social work supervision, staff development, and consultation will be reviewed. Consideration will be given to the similarities and differences in the roles, knowledge and skills required, emphasizing the teaching–learning–evaluating components. Issues arising from organizational settings, changing legislation and program provisions, and professional standards will be identified and examined.

While supervision, staff development, and consultation have a long history in social work, there is ambiguity about how practitioners are best prepared to do any of these roles. Unfortunately, too few people prepare at all. This course will provide theory and techniques to improve social work practice. This will be achieved through readings, discussions, role playing, case examples, and special assignments using videotapes and other media. The textbooks that will be used for this course are:

Middleman, Ruth, and Rhodes, Gary. *Competent Supervision*. Englewood Cliffs, N.J.: Prentice Hall Inc., 1985.

Austin, Michael, Bannon, Deanne, and Pecora, Peter. *Managing Staff Development Programs in Human Service Agencies*. Chicago: Nelson-Hall Publishers, 1984.

Additional reading for the various subjects will be provided by the instructor for circulation among the class members. The specifically assigned readings for each week are found after the description of the lecture-discussion concepts for each date. A short bibliography of pertinent citations is appended to the Course Schedule. Students are encouraged to use these citations to follow up on subjects that are of particular interest or relevance to their individual professional development. It is expected of graduate students that assigned readings are completed by the appropriate class period. This is particularly important in a class that meets just once per week.

COURSE CONTENT AND METHODOLOGY

The course is devoted to the management function of teaching personnel through the three most common modes in social work practice: staff development, supervision, and consultation. Of these three, supervision receives greatest emphasis. The methodology will be varied and somewhat dependent on the interests of the class members. The initial plan will be for each meeting to contain both didactic and experiential learning. Liberal use will be made of written and media case examples.

EXPECTATIONS AND ASSIGNMENTS

Since the time element in this course is crucial, students will be expected to do readings in advance and be prepared to initiate discussion in the areas of interest.

Written assignments will consist of one major project, either in personnel supervision or in staff development, and a written final examination, essay format, which will focus on practice applications of the principles and techniques discussed during the semester.

The suggested format for the major papers and way of approaching this assignment will be discussed as the course content progresses. For specific dates, refer to the Course Schedule.

Grades will be assigned on the following basis:

- 20% class participation and presentation of readings
- 40% supervision/staff development project
- 40% comprehensive problem-solving experience.

COURSE SCHEDULE

August 28
    1. Overview of class; discussion of management concepts; analysis of management as a process; supervision and personnel motivation.
        Course Syllabus
        Class Handouts

September 11
> **2.** The principles of adult learning; the process of educational evaluation; constant structuring and choice of methodologies; teaching techniques in adult education.
>> Middleman/Rhodes—Chapter 1: "Getting Oriented"
>> Kadushin—"Administrative Supervision"

September 18
> **3.** Structuring the educational supervision relationship; definition of functions; methodology of assessment; ordering content and choosing a teaching method.
>> Middleman/Rhodes—Chapter 2
>> Kadushin—"A Diagnosis for Almost All Occasions"

September 25
> **4.** Principles of individual supervision; models in the use of the case conference as a teaching mechanism; sex role issues in supervision.
>> Mandell, Betty—"The 'Equality' Revolution and Supervision"
>> Rosenblatt, Aaron, and Mayer, John—"Objectionable Supervisory Styles: Students' Views"
>> Abrahamson, Arthur—"The Professional Development of the Supervisor"

October 2
> **5.** Use of the staff group as mechanism for supervision; peer group supervision, advantages and limitations; common uses of group methodology in tasks of personnel management.
>> Middleman/Rhodes—Chapter 3
>> Hare and Frankens—"Peer Group Supervision"
>> Pettes, Dorothy—"Group Supervision"

October 9
> **6.** Supervision in the crisis context of the social agency; the principles of crisis intervention strategy applied to the supervisory function.
>> Middleman/Rhodes—Chapter 4
>> Eaton, Joseph—"Stress in Social Work Practice"
>> Schour, Esther—"Helping Social Workers Handle Work Stress"

October 16
> **7.** Workload management and the supervisory function; case classification techniques; time and effort weighting and the assessment process.
>> Middleman/Rhodes—Chapter 5
>> Pettes, Dorothy—"Management Tasks Related to Individual Workers"

Hunsicher, Frank—"How to Approach Communications Difficulties"

Muson, Carlton—"Professional Autonomy and Social Work Supervision"

October 23

8. Trouble-shooting the work group; common personal problems and their solutions; source of work disruption and employee dissatisfaction; ethical considerations in racial and ethnic issues of supervision.

Middleman/Rhodes—Chapter 6

October 30

9. The evaluating function; personnel evaluation vs. performance evaluation; the evaluation process and its relationship to the teaching function; issues of discrimination in personnel and performance evaluation.

Middleman/Rhodes—Chapter 7

Stapleton, Richard C.—"Terminations: Lower-Level Terminations"

November 6

10. Managing a volunteer program; components, recruitment, selection, training, supervising, and rewarding volunteers; accountability in volunteerism.

Middleman/Rhodes—Chapter 8

Ulm—"Volunteers in Corrections," *Staff Manual*

November 13

11. Staff training and staff development; organization and personal goals; types of training programs; functions performed by the staff development personnel.

Austin, et al.—Chapters 1, 2, and 3

Campbell—"Methodology of Training Evaluation"

Podnos, Ira—"The 'Consultative' Method of Training"

November 20

12. Steps in developing a staff development program; learning needs assessment; establishing goals, ordering content, choosing methodology; teaching techniques; evaluating program outcomes.

Austin, et al.—Chapters 4, 5, and 6

Bauby, Cathy—"The Leader's Role in Role Playing"

Garzino, Salvatore—"Objective Tests in Training"

Weiss, Carol H.—"Evolution of Staff Training Programs"

November 27
   13. Consultation as adult education; differential types of consultation based on goals and process; generic steps of the consultation process.
      Middleman/Rhodes—Chapter 9
      Cook—"Ten Commandments of Consultation"

December 4
   14. Entry tasks in consultation; assessment, goal determination, and developing the consultation contract; motives in seeking consultation; contextual factors influencing consultative process.
      Green, Rose—"The Consultant and the Consultation Process"
      Leader, Arthur L.—"Supervision and Consultation Through Observed Interviewing"
      Roberts, Robert—"Some Impressions of Mental Health Consultation in a Poverty Area"

December 11
   15. Course summary and evaluation; examination discussion.

SUPPLEMENTAL READINGS

1. Staff Development and Training

Campbell, John, and Dunnette, Marvin. *Managerial Behavior, Performance and Effectiveness.* New York: McGraw Hill, 1970. Chapter 10, "Training and Development: Methods and Techniques," pp. 233–52; and Chapter 11, "Applications of Basic Research and Theory," pp. 253–70.

Doelker, R. E. "Strategies in Staff Development: An Ecological Approach," *Social Work,* 28:380–84 October 1983.

Frey, Louise, Shatz, Eunice, and Katz, Edna Ann. "Continuing Education—Teaching Staff to Teach," *Social Casework,* vol. 55, no. 6 (June 1974), pp. 360–368.

Jones, R. L. "Increasing Staff Sensitivity to the Black Client," *Social Casework,* 64:419–25, September 1983.

Kagan, R. M. "Staff Development for a Therapeutic Environment," *Child Welfare,* 62:203–11, June 1983.

Lauffer, Armand. *The Practice of Continuing Education in Human Services.* New York: McGraw Hill, 1977. Chapter 13, "Program Evaluation," pp. 175–89.

Lauffer, Armand, and Sturdevant, Celeste. *Doing Continuing Education and Staff Development.* New York: McGraw Hill, 1977. Assignments will be made later.

Maluccio, Anthony N. "Staff Development in Child Welfare: A Review of Recent Literature," *Child and Youth Services,* vol. 1, no. 3 (May/June 1977), pp. 1, 3–9.

Montavolo, F. F. "Training Child Welfare Workers for Cultural Awareness: The Culture Simulator Technique," *Child Welfare,* 61:341–53, June 1982.

Nadler, Leonard, and Nadler, Zeace. *The Conference Book*. Houston: Gulf Publishing Co., 1977. (How to design, plan, staff, and run conferences of 20 or more people.)

Patti, Rino, and Rearick, Herman. "The Dynamics of Agency Change," *Social Casework,* vol. 53, no. 4 (April 1972), pp. 243–55. (Note: The entire April 1972 issue of *Social Casework* is devoted to aspects of staff development in family agencies.)

Pecora, P. J. "Assessing Worker Training Needs: Use of Staff Surveys and Key Informant Interviews," *Child Welfare,* 62:395–407, October 1983.

Rothman, Beulah. "Perspectives on Learning and Teaching in Continuing Education," *Journal of Education for Social Work,* vol. 9, no. 2 (Spring 1973), pp. 39–52.

Swack, Lois. "Continuing Education and Changing Needs," *Social Work,* vol. 20, no. 6 (November 1975), pp. 474–80.

Waltz, Thomas. "A Continuing Education Curriculum for the Graduate Social Worker," *Journal of Education for Social Work,* vol. 9, no. 1 (Winter 1973), pp. 68–78.

Weiss, Carol H. *Evaluation Research*. Englewood Cliffs, N.J.: Prentice Hall, 1972, pp. 1–9 and 26–84.

2. Supervision

Austin, C. E. "Experiences of Women as Social Welfare Administrators," *Social Work,* 30:173–9, April 1985.

Austin, Lucille N. "Basic Principles of Supervision," in Munson, *Classic Statements,* pp. 56–69.

Berl, Fred. "An Attempt to Construct a Conceptual Framework for Supervision," in Munson, *Classic Statements,* pp. 94–105.

Brieland, Donald, Briggs, Thomas, and Leuenberger, Paul. *The Team Model of Social Work Practice*. Syracuse, N.Y.: Syracuse University Press, 1973.

Bruner, Jerome. *The Process of Education*. New York: Vintage Books, 1963. Particularly Chapters 2 and 3, pp. 17–54.

Campbell, John, et al. *Managerial Behavior, Performance and Effectiveness*. New York: McGraw Hill, 1970. Particularly Chapter 5, "Divining and Measuring Managerial Effectiveness," pp. 101–26, and Chapter 12, "The Methodology of Training Evaluation," pp. 271–86.

Finch, Wilbur A. "The Role of the Organization," Chapter 3 in Kaslow et al., *Supervision, Consultation, and Staff Training in the Helping Professions*. Florence Whiteman Kaslow and Assoc., San Francisco: Jossey-Bass Publishers, 1977, pp. 282–301.

Findale, Ruth. "Peer Group Supervision," *Social Casework,* vol. 34, no. 8 (October 1958), pp. 443–50. (Munson, pp. 122–32).

Fueckler, Merle, and Deutschberger, Paul. "Growth-Oriented Supervision," *Public Welfare,* vol. 28, no. 3 (July 1970), pp. 297–302.

Getzel, G., Goldbert, J., and Salmon, R. "Supervising in Groups as a Model for Today," *Social Casework,* vol. 52, no. 3 (March 1971), pp. 154–63.

Granvold, Donald K. "Training Social Work Supervisors to Meet Organizational and Worker Objectives," *Journal of Education for Social Work,* vol. 14, no. 2 (Spring 1978), pp. 38–45.

Henning, Margaret, and Jardim, Anne. *The Managerial Woman*. New York: Pocket Books, 1977.

Jayaratne, S., and Chess, W. A. "Job Satisfaction, Burnout, and Turnover: A National Study," *Social Work*, 29:448–53, October 1984.

Kadushin, Alfred. "Supervisor–Supervisee: A Survey," in Munson, *Classic Statements*, pp. 244–57.

Kaslow, F. W., et al. *Supervision, Consultation, and Staff Training in the Helping Professions*. San Francisco: Jossey-Bass, 1977.

Kutzik, Alfred. "Class and Ethnic Factors," in F. W. Kaslow, *Issues in Human Services*. San Francisco: Jossey-Bass, 1972, pp. 85–114.

Levy, Charles. "The Ethics of Supervision," *Social Work*, vol. 18, no. 2 (March 1973), pp. 14–21. (Munson, pp. 216–26)

Levy, Charles. *Social Work Ethics*. New York: Human Sciences Press, 1976.

Miller, Irving. "Supervision in Social Work," in *Encyclopedia of Social Work* (17th issue). New York: National Association of Social Workers, 1977, pp. 1544–51.

Munson, Carlton, *Social Work Supervision: Classic Statements and Critical Issues*. New York: The Free Press, 1979.

Nelsen, Judith. "Teaching Content of Early Field Work Conference," *Social Casework*, vol. 55, no. 3 (March 1974), pp. 147–53.

Olmstead, Joseph A., and Christensen, Harold E. "Study of Agency Work Contexts: Implications for Supervision," *Program Application Report No. 1*. Washington, D.C.: Department of Health, Education and Welfare (SRS) 74-05405, 1973, pp. 1–17.

Perlmutter, Felice. "Barometer of Professional Change," in F. W. Kaslow, *Issues in Human Services*. San Francisco: Jossey-Bass, 1972, pp. 1–17.

Royster, Eugene. "Black Supervisors: Problems of Race and Role," in F. W. Kaslow, *Issues in Human Services*. San Francisco: Jossey-Bass, 1972, pp. 72–84.

Scherz, Frances H. "A Concept of Supervision Based on Definitions of Job Responsibility," in Munson, *Classic Statements*, pp. 7–82.

Stewart, Nathaniel. *The Effective Woman Manager: Seven Vital Skills for Upward Mobility*. New York: Wiley, 1978.

Sutton, J. A. "Sex Discrimination Among Social Workers," *Social Work*, 27:211–17, May 1982.

Timberlake, E. M. "Peer Group Supervision for Supervisors," *Social Casework*, 63:82–87, February 1982.

Weinbach, R. W. "Implementing Change: Insights and Strategies for the Supervisor," *Social Work*, 29:282–86, June 1984.

Wilson, Susanna. *Confidentiality in Social Work: Issues and Principles*. New York: The Free Press, 1978.

Wolf, J. H. "Professionalizing" Volunteer Work in Black Neighborhoods," *Social Service Review*, 59:423–34 September 1985.

3. Consultation

Bermont, Robert. *How to Become a Successful Consultant in Your Own Field*. Washington, D.C.: Bermont Books, 1978.

Caplan, Gerald. *The Theory and Practice of Mental Health Consultation*. New York: Basic Books, 1970. (This is an excellent book to purchase for your own library.)

Collins, Alice H., Pancoast, Diane L., and Dunn, June. *Consultation Casebook*. Portland, Ore.: Portland State University, February 1977. Handout.

Cook, Maxwell. "Ten Commandments of Consultation," *Public Welfare*. vol. 28, no. 3 (July 1970), pp. 303–5.

Costin, Lela. "Supervision and Consultation in the Licensing of Family Homes: The Use of Non-Professional Personnel," *Child Welfare,* January 1967, pp. 10–15.

Larsen, Judith K., Morris, Eleanor L., and Kroll, John. *Consultation and Its Outcome: Community Mental Health Centers*. Palo Alto, Cal.: American Institute for Research, 1976.

Mannino, Fortune, MacLennan, Beryce, and Shore, Milton. *The Practice of Mental Health Consultation*. Washington, D.C.: National Institute of Mental Health, U.S. Department of Health, Education and Welfare, Superintendent of Documents, U.S. Government Printing Office, 1975. Chapter 1, "Mental Health Consultation: Definition, Scope and Effects," pp. 3–48.

Margulies, Newton, and Wallace, John. *Organizational Change: Techniques and Applications*. Glenview, Ill.: Scott, Foresman and Co., 1973.

Rapoport, Lydia, ed. *Consultation in Social Work Practice*. New York: National Association of Social Workers, 1963.

Watkins, Elizabeth L., Holland, Thomas F., and Ritvo, Roger. "Improving the Effectiveness of Program Consultation," *Social Work in Health Care,* vol. 2, no. 1 (Fall 1976), pp. 43–54.

Webb, N. B. "Crisis Consultation: Preventive Implications," *Social Casework,* 62:465–71, April 1981.

Saint Louis University
School of Social Service

Supervision and Consultation as Social Work Practice

Instructor
Dr. John J. Stretch

COURSE DESCRIPTION

The purpose of this course is to enable the student to conceptualize, assess, and apply supervision and consultation as facilitative forms of generic social work practice.

COURSE OBJECTIVES

The objectives of the course are to:

1. Understand the historical and current relationship of supervision and consultation to social work practice.
2. Understand organizational context as it enhances or delimits the effectiveness of social work supervision and consultation practice.
3. Understand policy and practice issues surrounding supervision and consultation as these influence administrative, teaching, and collaborative functions inherent in social work supervision and consultation.
4. Enhance the skill level of the student in the utilization of supervision and consultation models and approaches in social work practice.
5. Examine current ethical issues of social work supervision and consultation.
6. Integrate research findings on the process and impact of social work

supervision and consultation as developing modes of social work practice.

7. Assess future trends in the practice of social work supervision and consultation.

REQUIRED TEXTS

Michael J. Austin. *Supervisory Management for the Human Services*. Englewood Cliffs, N.J.: Prentice Hall, 1981.

Carlton E. Munson. *An Introduction to Clinical Social Work Supervision*. New York: Hawthorne Press. 1983.

Lawrence Shulman. *Skills of Supervision and Staff Management*. Itasca, Ill.: F.E. Peacock, 1982.

Sessions	*Required Reading*
1	Introduction to Course
2	Shulman 1
3	Shulman 2
4	Austin 1 and 2
5	Austin 3 and 4
6	Shulman 3
7	Shulman 4
8	Austin 5
9	Austin 6 and 7
10	Shulman 5
11	Shulman 6
12	Austin 8
13	Shulman 7
14	Austin 9
15	Austin 10
16	Student presentations

SUPPLEMENTAL REFERENCES AND AUTHORS

The Munson text and the Shulman text have extensive bibliographies on the literature on supervision and consultation. The range is from the pioneering works of the charity organization society in the early 1900s to current conceptual and empirical work of the 1980s. For very recent literature the student should consult 1980–1985 issues of *Social Work Research and Abstracts* under the main entries of "Supervision" and "Consultation."

COURSE DESCRIPTION
AND MAJOR ASSIGNMENT

The course will consist of readings, discussions, and exercises. Because of the seminar nature of the course and the mutual learning and reinforcement of skills which are desired in the course, students are expected to attend each session and be prepared to elaborate on and critique what is being discussed both from the literature in the field as well as from their own professional experience.

A major individual paper of between sixteen and twenty pages which focuses on supervisory strategy or consultation approach(es) integrated through a case analysis or a theoretical model will provide the major integration of material learned in the course. Papers are due the last class period. Papers should be typewritten and follow the usual style of professional journal writing. An annotated bibliography must be included.

A brief prospectus on one of two typewritten pages with necessary documentation and literature should be turned in for instructive review and feedback by the fourth class session. Each student will present his/her paper to the class for discussion and assessment. It is not necessary for the paper to be a finished product at the time of presentation.

COURSE GRADING SYSTEM

The course will be graded on the following basis:

4.0	A	100–90
3.5	B+	89–85
3.0	B	84–80
2.5	C+	79–75
2.0	C	74–70
0		69 and below

The grade will be weighed as follows:

Class Participation	20%
Class Presentation	20%
Final Paper	60%

Index

A113   0746563 0

HV 689 .R54 1991

Rieman, Dwight W.

Strategies in social work
 consultation